A Beginning Look at Canada

A N N E - M A R I E   K A S K E N S

Toronto Catholic School Board
Continuing Education Department

Prentice Hall Allyn and Bacon Canada
Scarborough, Ontario

Canadian Cataloguing in Publication Data

Kaskens, Anne-Marie
    A beginning look at Canada

ISBN 0–13–760117–4

1. English language – Textbooks for second language learners.* 2. Readers – Canada. I. Title.

PE1128.K37 1998   428.6′4   C97–930574–8

© 1998 Prentice-Hall Canada Inc., Scarborough, Ontario
A Division of Simon & Schuster/A Viacom Company

Prentice-Hall, Inc., Upper Saddle River, New Jersey
Prentice-Hall International (UK) Limited, London
Prentice-Hall of Australia, Pty. Limited, Sydney
Prentice-Hall Hispanoamericana, S.A., Mexico City
Prentice-Hall of India Private Limited, New Delhi
Prentice-Hall of Japan, Inc., Tokyo
Simon & Schuster Southeast Asia Private Limited, Singapore
Editora Prentice-Hall do Brasil, Ltda., Rio de Janeiro

ISBN 0–13–760117–4

Acquisitions Editor: Dominique Roberge
Developmental Editor: Marta Tomins
Copy Editor: Sharon Kirsch
Production Editor: Mary Ann McCutcheon
Editorial Assistant: Ivetka Vasil
Production Coordinator: Jane Schell
Permissions/Photo Research: Marijke Leupen
Cover Design: Mary Opper
Cover Image: The Painted Flag #31 by Charles Pachter, acrylic on canvas, 1981
Page Design and Layout: Gail Ferreira Ng-A-Kien
Illustrator: William Kimber

2 3 4 5   BBG   02 01 00 99 98

Printed and bound in the United States

Visit the Prentice Hall Canada Web site! Send us your comments, browse our catalogues, and more. **www.phcanada.com**. Or reach us through e-mail at **phabinfo_pubcanada@prenhall.com**

Statistics Canada data on pages 75, 77, 81, 87, 90 and 99 are adapted from and reproduced by authority of the Minister of Industry, 1997, Statistics Canada.

Data on page 38 are adapted from and reproduced with the permission of the Minister of Public Works and Government Services Canada, 1997.

Photo Credits

Page 29, PH Canada Archives; page 32, © Canadian Tourism Commission; page 35, PH Canada Archives; page 46 (top), Tom Hanson/Canapress; (bottom), © Canadian Tourism Commission; page 58, BCARS/77304; page 61 (top), Courtesy Canadian Heritage; (bottom), NAC/C-141503; page 67 (top), Alex Urosevic/Toronto Sun; page 67 (bottom right), Canada Post Corporation; page 67 (bottom left), Royal Canadian Mint; page 69, National Capital Commission; page 81, Al Harvey; page 93 (top) and page 94 (top left), PH Canada Archives; page 93 (second from top) and page 94 (top right), Dick Hemingway; page 93 (second from bottom) and page 94 (bottom left), PH Canada Archives; page 93 (bottom) and page 94 (bottom right), Al Harvey; page 97, PH Canada Archives; page 105, Reproduced with the permission of the Treasury Board of Canada Secretariat, 1997; page 108, Courtesy Elections Canada; page 111 (top right), Jean-Marc Carisse, Office of the Prime Minister; page 111 (bottom), Courtesy Elections Canada; page 113, Courtesy Elections Canada; page 113 (bottom), Courtesy Elections Canada; page 119, Hamilton Spectator/Canapress; page 121 (top), National Capital Commission; (bottom), PH Canada Archives; page 123 (from left to right), Progressive Conservative Party of Canada; The New Democrats; Reform Party of Canada; and Leader of the Opposition; page 131, Jean-Marc Carisse, Office of the Prime Minister; page 134, PH Canada Archives; page 136, Government House, Ottawa; page 142, Courtesy Elections Canada; page 143 (top and bottom), © Canadian Tourism Commission; page 151, Jean-Marc Carisse, Office of the Prime Minister; page 154, Stan Behal/Toronto Sun.

Table of Contents

Preface vi

PART 1—THE LAND   1

Getting Ready to Learn 2

Unit 1   The Size of Canada 4

Unit 2   Provinces and Territories 7

Unit 3   Capital Cities 11

Unit 4   Driving Across Canada 14

Unit 5   Oceans and Great Lakes 17

Unit 6   Regions of Canada 20

Unit 7   The Atlantic Region .22

Unit 8   Central Canada 26

Unit 9   The Prairie Provinces 29

Unit 10 The West Coast 32

Unit 11 The North 35

Unit 12 The Weather 38

Glossary **41**

PART 2—THE HISTORY   43

Getting Ready to Learn **44**

Unit 1   The First Peoples 46

Unit 2   The Early Settlers 49

Unit 3   British Rule 52

Unit 4   Confederation 55

Unit 5   Settling the West 58

Unit 6   The Constitution Act 61

Unit 7   The First Peoples Today 64

Unit 8   Celebrating Our History 67

Glossary **71**

PART 3—THE PEOPLE
73

Getting Ready to Learn **74**

Unit 1   The Population of Canada 75

Unit 2   The Populations of Other Countries 79

Unit 3   Where Canadians Live 81

Unit 4   Who Canadians Are 84

Unit 5   Immigration 87

Unit 6   Languages Canadians Speak 90

Unit 7   Canadians and Work 93

Unit 8   Canadians Help Each Other 97

Glossary **100**

PART 4—THE GOVERNMENT
101

Getting Ready to Learn **103**

Unit 1   The Levels of Government 104

Unit 2   Canada Is a Democracy 108

Unit 3   An Election 111

Unit 4   How We Vote 113

The Federal Government **116**

Unit 5   Ridings 116

Unit 6   Members of Parliament 119

Unit 7   House of Commons 121

Unit 8   Political Parties 123

Unit 9   The Prime Minister 125

Unit 10 Prime Ministers of Canada 129

Unit 11 The Cabinet 131

Unit 12 The Senate 134

Unit 13 The Governor General 136

Unit 14 Summary 138

The Provincial Government **139**

Unit 15 Ridings 139

Unit 16 Members of the Provincial Government 142

Unit 17 Political Parties 147

Unit 18 The Premier 148

Unit 19 The Cabinet 151
Unit 20 The Lieutenant Governor 154
Unit 21 Summary 157
Unit 22 The Municipal Government 159
Unit 23 Members of the Municipal Government 161
Glossary **164**

Preface

A *Beginning Look at Canada* is for teachers who want to teach fundamental facts and concepts about Canada while providing reading and writing practice.

A *Beginning Look at Canada* is for learners who want to learn about Canada while improving their reading and writing skills.

Many adults lack a basic understanding of the workings of Canadian government, of our history and our geography. Many books assume a background knowledge of Canada. For the reader who lacks this background knowledge, reading such books is a frustrating and intimidating process. Other learners have reading difficulties that make reading at higher levels strenuous, yet many books written for these learners offer little content.

This text is particularly useful to beginning learners of English as a Second Language who are interested in learning about Canada. It is also useful to other adult learners and students in the school system. Selected facts and events have been chosen so the reader is not overwhelmed by detail. The text provides an overview of Canada, a sense of the "big picture." Often learners need a sense of the whole before learning about the specific. This text tries to fill that need.

Organization of the Text

The text contains four parts: **The Land, The History, The People** and **The Government.** Each part includes a number of short units, from two to five pages in length. Each unit begins with a reading followed by comprehension exercises.

Pre-Reading and Glossary

Each part is preceded by a pre-reading exercise titled **Getting Ready to Learn** and ends with a **Glossary**. The pre-reading exercise helps the learner focus his or her attention on the material. It triggers prior learning about the subject and allows the learner to set his or her own learning goals. The glossary of terms reviews the vocabulary of the part.

Readings

There are 53 readings, each followed by comprehension exercises. The purpose of the readings is to present information about Canada in a sequential, easy-to-understand format.

Most readings are limited to one page and provide the content for the units. The sentences are short, and the text does not assume a background knowledge of Canada.

Bolded key terms, unit headings, subheadings, maps, tables and illustrations are included to help the learner make sense of the text.

Where possible, the sentence structure and grammar are kept simple. The present and simple past tenses are common. Usually the beginning-level ESL learner has not yet learned complex tenses, and for some learners with reading difficulties, complex sentence structure obscures meaning.

Comprehension Exercises

Each reading is followed by a number of exercises. Learners read material in short spells, then practise it right away. The comprehension exercises serve as self-testing for learners, allowing them to confirm their learning frequently.

Some of the exercises are easy to complete, whereas others are more challenging. There is also some repetition. This is intentional. Repeated exposure to information in different contexts is an important part of the learning process. Success builds confidence and motivation for learning. It is the intention that learners "overlearn" some basic concepts about Canada, so they can build and retain a knowledge base.

A number of different exercises appear throughout the text. They are titled **Word Meanings, Match, Order, Fill in the Blanks, Circle the Correct Answer, True or False, Answer the Questions, Writing, Sort, Crossword Puzzles** and **Discuss.**

They focus on the content of the reading and include prompting the learner to scan or re-read the text for specific details; to interpret charts and maps; to answer true or false questions; to order information chronologically; to categorize and organize material; to recall key facts; and to match new vocabulary with meanings. The exercises provide the learner with reading and writing practice, and help the learner build and retain a vocabulary and background knowledge about Canada.

The exercises can be completed in a variety of ways. Students can work individually— in class or for homework—or in pairs or small groups. There is an answer key in the Teacher's Manual.

Teacher's Manual and Resource Package

The Teacher's Manual and Resource Package includes learning outcomes in checklist form, pre-reading suggestions for introducing each unit, photocopiable masters for making flashcards, and an answer key for the comprehension exercises.

Acknowledgments

I would like to thank Mark Brender for his enthusiasm, encouragement and suggestions. I would also like to thank Jane Hill, from W. A. Porter Collegiate, and Fran Marshall, from Etobicoke ESL, for reviewing the manuscript.

PART **1**
The Land

Getting Ready to Learn 2

UNIT 1   The Size of Canada 4

UNIT 2   Provinces and Territories 7

UNIT 3   Capital Cities 11

UNIT 4   Driving Across Canada .14

UNIT 5   Oceans and Great Lakes 17

UNIT 6   Regions of Canada 20

UNIT 7   The Atlantic Region 22

UNIT 8   Central Canada 26

UNIT 9   The Prairie Provinces .29

UNIT 10 The West Coast 32

UNIT 11 The North 35

UNIT 12 The Weather 38

Glossary 41

In Part 1 you will learn about Canada's land. Before you work on the units, answer these questions.

1. Do you think Canada is a big country compared with other countries in the world?
2. Do you like the weather in Canada?
3. Where would you like to live? In the north? Near the water? In a big city or in a small town? Why?
4. Find Canada on the map. Find another country you have visited or lived in. Is this country bigger than Canada? Do you think it has more people than Canada? Did you cross an ocean to get to Canada? Which ocean did you cross?
5. On the map write the names of any other countries you know.

GETTING READY TO LEARN

Think about the topics listed in the left-hand column. In the middle column, write what you already know about the topics. Then write three things you want to find out about the topics in the right-hand column.

ABOUT	I ALREADY KNOW	I WANT TO FIND OUT
the size of Canada		1. _____ 2. _____ 3. _____
Canada's provinces and territories		1. _____ 2. _____ 3. _____
the population of Canada		1. _____ 2. _____ 3. _____
the weather in Canada		1. _____ 2. _____ 3. _____

Read

Canada is a large country. It is about 4 600 kilometres from north to south, and about 5 500 kilometres from east to west.

Is Canada the Biggest Country in the World?

Canada is not the biggest country in the world. It is the second-biggest country in the world. The biggest country in the world is Russia.

Where Is Canada?

A **continent** is a huge area of land. There are seven continents in the world. Canada is on the continent of **North America**.

There are three countries in North America: Canada, the United States and Mexico. Canada is north of the United States.

COUNTRIES BY SIZE	
Biggest	Russia
Second	Canada
Third	China
Fourth	United States
Fifth	Brazil
Sixth	Australia

Understand What You Read

A. Fill in the Blanks

Use the words in the box.

> **the largest • the second-largest • the third-largest
> the fourth-largest • the fifth-largest • the sixth-largest**

1. China is _____ country in the world.

2. Australia is _____ country in the world.

3. Russia is _____ country in the world.

4. Canada is _____ country in the world.

5. The United States is _____ country in the world.

6. Brazil is _____ country in the world.

B. Answer the Questions

1. What is a continent?

   _____

2. How many continents are there in the world?

   _____

3. Name three countries in North America.

   _____

4. How long is Canada from north to south?

   _____

5. How wide is Canada from east to west?

   _____

Understand What You Read

C. Circle the Correct Answer

1. Canada is the
   - a) smallest country in the world
   - b) largest country in the world
   - c) second-largest country in the world

2. Canada is north of
   - a) Russia
   - b) Brazil
   - c) the United States

3. The largest country in the world is
   - a) Russia
   - b) Canada
   - c) China

D. Crossword Puzzle

Down

1. The third-biggest country
2. The sixth-biggest country
5. Australia is the _____ biggest country
8. Brazil is the _____ biggest country
9. Canada is the _____ biggest country

Across

1. The second-biggest country
3. China is the _____ biggest country
4. The fourth-biggest country
6. The biggest country in the world
7. The fifth-biggest country

Read

Canada is divided into 10 provinces and two territories. The names of the provinces and territories are on the map.

East and West

British Columbia is at the **western** end of Canada. Newfoundland is at the **eastern** end of Canada. Canada's two territories are in the North of Canada.

Biggest and Smallest

Quebec is the biggest province in Canada. Prince Edward Island is the smallest province.

Understand What You Read

A. Fill in the Blanks

Write the provinces and territories on the map.

1. There are _____ provinces in Canada.

2. There are _____ territories in Canada.

3. The smallest province is _____.

4. The biggest province is _____.

Understand What You Read

B. Fill in the Blanks

Use the words in the box.

smaller than • bigger than • biggest • smallest

1. New Brunswick is _____ _____ Ontario.

2. Manitoba is _____ _____ Nova Scotia.

3. Alberta is _____ _____ Prince Edward Island.

4. Prince Edward Island is the _____ province in Canada.

5. Quebec is the _____ province in Canada.

6. The Northwest Territories is the _____ territory in Canada.

C. Fill in the Blanks

north • south • east • west

1. The Yukon Territory is _____ of Alberta.

2. Ontario is _____ of Quebec.

3. Newfoundland is _____ of Prince Edward Island.

4. Nova Scotia is _____ of Ontario.

5. New Brunswick is _____ of Nova Scotia.

6. British Columbia is _____ of the Yukon Territory.

7. British Columbia is _____ of Saskatchewan.

8. Saskatchewan is _____ of Manitoba.

Understand What You Read

D. Fill in the Blanks

The short form of each province or territory is listed below. Write the name of the correct province or territory beside its short form.

Northwest Territories	**Prince Edward Island**	**Nova Scotia**
Saskatchewan	**Newfoundland**	**Yukon Territory**
British Columbia	**Manitoba**	**New Brunswick**
Ontario	**Alberta**	**Quebec**

B.C. _____

Alta. _____

Sask. _____

Man. _____

Ont. _____

Que. _____

Nfld. _____

N.B. _____

N.S. _____

P.E.I. _____

Y.T. _____

N.W.T. _____

E. Discuss

1. How many provinces in Canada have you visited?

2. Name another country that is divided into different provinces or parts.

3. Why do you think a country is divided into provinces?

Read

What Is a Capital City?

There are hundreds of cities in Canada, but there are only 13 **capital cities**. Canada has a capital city, and each province or territory in Canada also has a capital city. Governments do their work in capital cities.

The capital of Canada is **Ottawa**. It appears beside a small square on the map.

The capital of each province or territory appears beside a small circle on the map.

Understand What You Read

A. Fill in the Blanks

Find the capital cities on the map on page 11. Then write each capital city beside its province or territory.

Yellowknife	Charlottetown	Halifax
Regina	St. John's	Whitehorse
Victoria	Winnipeg	Fredericton
Toronto	Edmonton	Quebec City

PROVINCE OR TERRITORY	CAPITAL CITY
British Columbia	_____
Alberta	_____
Saskatchewan	_____
Manitoba	_____
Ontario	_____
Quebec	_____
Newfoundland	_____
New Brunswick	_____
Nova Scotia	_____
Prince Edward Island	_____
Yukon Territory	_____
Northwest Territories	_____

Understand What You Read

B. Fill in the Blanks

Use the words in the box.

| is • is not |

1. British Columbia _____ a province.

2. Charlottetown _____ a province.

3. Halifax _____ a capital city.

4. Edmonton _____ a province.

5. Prince Edward Island _____ a capital city.

6. Fredericton _____ a capital city.

7. Fredericton _____ the capital city of British Columbia.

8. Halifax _____ the capital city of Nova Scotia.

9. Winnipeg _____ the capital city of Prince Edward Island.

10. Whitehorse _____ the capital city of Northwest Territories.

11. Toronto _____ the capital city of Quebec.

12. Regina _____ the capital city of Saskatchewan.

C. Answer the Questions

1. What is the capital city of Canada? _____

2. What is the capital city of the province you live in? _____

3. How many capital cities are in Canada? _____

4. Who has meetings in the capital city? _____

5. What is the capital city of Canada's smallest province? _____

Read

A highway crosses Canada from the east to the west. It is called the **TransCanada Highway.**
From Vancouver, British Columbia, to Halifax, Nova Scotia, it is 5 840 **kilometres** long.

What Is a Kilometre?

A kilometre measures distance. A kilometre is about 10 city blocks.

In Canada we measure length in centimetres, metres and kilometres. They are part of the **metric system**.

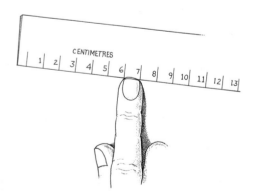

METRIC UNITS	
1 centimetre	is about the width of your fingernail
1 metre	is 100 centimetres
1 kilometre	is 1 000 metres

The United States measures distance in inches, feet, yards and miles. These are part of the **Imperial system.** It is different from the metric system.

In the past Canada used the Imperial system, but now we use the metric system.

Understand What You Read

A. Sort

Write the words under *Imperial* or *Metric*.

> Canada • feet • inches • miles • centimetres
> metres • United States • kilometres

IMPERIAL	METRIC
_____	_____
_____	_____
_____	_____
_____	_____

B. Answer the Questions

1. How many centimetres are in a metre? _____

2. How many metres are in a kilometre? _____

3. Is a centimetre shorter than a metre? _____

4. Is a kilometre longer than a metre? _____

C. Discuss

1. How long do you think it takes to walk one kilometre?
2. How long do you think it takes to run one kilometre?
3. Why do you think Canada changed from using the Imperial system to using the metric system?

Understand What You Read

DRIVING DISTANCES BETWEEN CAPITAL CITIES WEST TO EAST

Victoria to Edmonton . . . . . .about 1 200 km

Edmonton to Regina . . . . .about 800 km

Regina to Winnipeg . . . . .about 600 km

Winnipeg to Toronto . . . . . .about 2 100 km

Toronto to Quebec City . . . . .about 800 km

Quebec City to Fredericton . . .about 700 km

Fredericton to Halifax . . . . . .about 400 km

*km means *kilometre*

D. Answer the Questions

You will drive 100 kilometres an hour.

1. You will drive from Victoria to Edmonton.

   About how many kilometres is it? _____

   How many hours will it take to get to Edmonton? _____

   Which direction will you drive in? _____

2. You will drive from Toronto to Winnipeg.

   About how many kilometres is it? _____

   How many hours will it take? _____

   Which direction will you drive in? _____

3. You will drive from Halifax to Quebec City.

   About how many kilometres is it? _____

   How many hours will it take? _____

   Which direction will you drive in? _____

4. You will drive from Halifax to Victoria.

   About how many kilometres is it? _____

   How many hours will it take? _____

   Which direction will you drive in? _____

Read

Great Lakes

Canada has five very big lakes. They are called the **Great Lakes**.
The Great Lakes are Lake Ontario, Lake Erie, Lake Huron, Lake Michigan and Lake Superior.

Oceans

Three oceans surround Canada. The Atlantic Ocean is east of Canada. The Pacific Ocean is west of Canada. The Arctic Ocean is north of Canada.

Oceans have salt water. Most lakes, including the Great Lakes, have fresh water.

Understand What You Read

A. Answer the Questions

1. Name the five Great Lakes.

   _____

   _____

   _____

   _____

   _____

2. Which ocean is east of Canada?

   _____

3. Which ocean is west of Canada?

   _____

4. Which ocean is north of Canada?

   _____

5. Name four provinces near the Atlantic Ocean.

   _____

   _____

   _____

   _____

6. Name one province near the Pacific Ocean.

   _____

7. Name one province near the Great Lakes.

   _____

8. Which Great Lake is mostly in the United States? _____

B. Fill in the Blanks

1. The _____ have salt water.

2. The _____ have fresh water.

Understand What You Read

C. True or False

Circle T or F. If the sentence is true, copy the sentence on the line. If the scentence is false, write a correct sentence on the line.

1. Canada has four Great Lakes.   T / F

   _____

2. There are five Great Lakes in Quebec.   T / F

   _____

3. The oceans have fresh water.   T / F

   _____

4. Each province has three capital cities.   T / F

   _____

5. The Great Lakes have salt water.   T / F

   _____

6. The Arctic Ocean is south of Canada.   T / F

   _____

7. Canada has four provinces on the Atlantic Ocean.   T / F

   _____

8. Canada has one province on the Pacific Ocean.   T / F

   _____

D. Discuss

1. Do you prefer to swim in an ocean or a lake? Why?
2. List some ocean fish and some lake fish.
3. Do you prefer to eat seafood or freshwater fish?
4. Which ocean do you think is the coldest? Why?

Read

Canada is often divided into five areas of land called **regions**. The land in each region is different from the other regions. The regions are

The Atlantic Region

Newfoundland • Prince Edward Island

Nova Scotia • New Brunswick

Central Canada

Quebec

Ontario

The Prairie Provinces

Manitoba • Saskatchewan • Alberta

The West Coast

British Columbia

The North

Northwest Territories • Yukon Territory

Understand What You Read

A. Fill in the Blanks

Write the correct provinces or territories under the regions. On each map shade the provinces or territories of each region.

The Atlantic Region

_____ • _____

_____ • _____

Central Canada

_____

_____

The Prairie Provinces

_____ • _____ • _____

The West Coast

_____

The North

_____ • _____

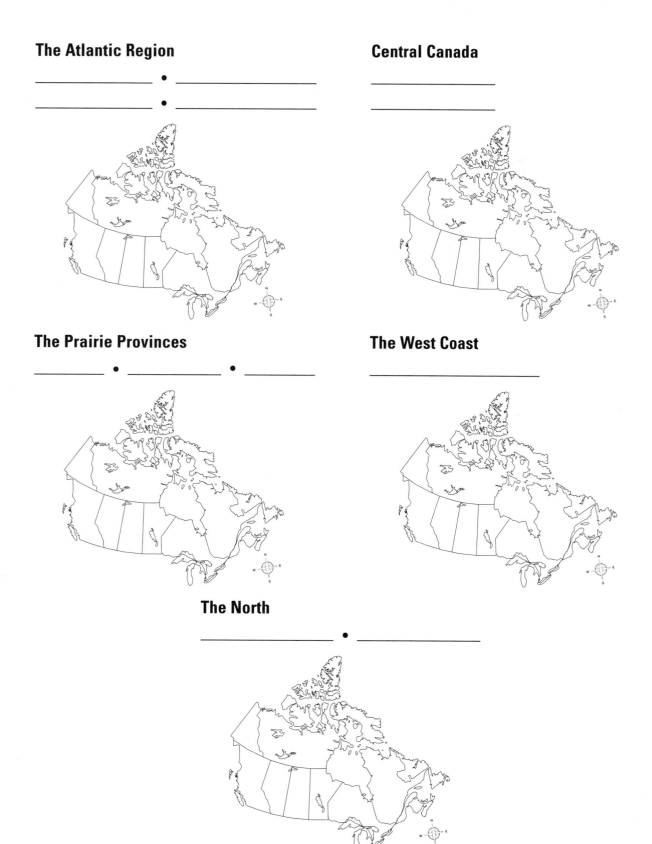

Read

Provinces

Newfoundland
Prince Edward Island
Nova Scotia
New Brunswick

Where Is the Atlantic Region?

The Atlantic region is next to the Atlantic Ocean. Some people call the Atlantic region the **Maritimes** or the **East Coast.** A coast is land right beside the ocean.

A Look at the Atlantic Region

The Atlantic region is smaller than the other regions of Canada. There are some farms, some cities and towns, and many small fishing villages. There are four provinces in the Atlantic region.

Newfoundland has two parts. The larger part is called *Labrador*. Newfoundland is mostly rocky with many small lakes and rivers. There are many fish in the coastal waters of Newfoundland.

Prince Edward Island is the smallest province in Canada. Most of the land is farmed. The farmers mostly grow potatoes.

Nova Scotia has two parts. The smaller part is an island called *Cape Breton Island*. Most of Nova Scotia is covered in forest. There are some farms and many small fishing villages.

New Brunswick is also covered mostly in forest. It has farms, and small cities and towns.

Compared with the Rest of Canada

The Atlantic region is smaller.
The Atlantic region has fewer cities.
The Atlantic region has a lower population.

Population is the number of people who live in a place.

Understand What You Read

A. Word Meanings

Write the correct words beside their meanings. Use the words in the box.

> **Atlantic region • coast • Labrador**
> **Cape Breton Island • population**

1. _____ part of Newfoundland

2. _____ the number of people who live in a place

3. _____ four provinces on the east side of Canada

4. _____ land next to the ocean

5. _____ a part of Nova Scotia

B. Answer the Questions

1. Name four provinces in the Atlantic region. Write the capital city of each province.

   Province   **Capital City**

   _____   _____

   _____   _____

   _____   _____

   _____   _____

2. Which two provinces in the Atlantic region have two parts?

   _____

3. What are two other names for the Atlantic region?

   _____

4. Which ocean is the Atlantic region close to?

   _____

Understand What You Read

C. Fill in the Blanks

Use the words in the box.

Newfoundland • Labrador • Nova Scotia • Cape Breton Island
New Brunswick • Prince Edward Island

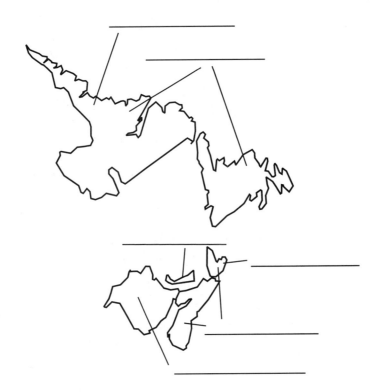

1. _____ is the smallest province in the Atlantic region.

2. _____ and _____ are next to Quebec.

3. _____ is the biggest province in the Atlantic region.

Understand What You Read

D. Fill in the Blanks

higher • larger • smaller • smallest • lower

1. The Atlantic region is _____ than the other regions in Canada.

2. Labrador is the _____ part of Newfoundland.

3. Cape Breton Island is the _____ part of Nova Scotia.

4. Prince Edward Island is _____ than Nova Scotia.

5. Prince Edward Island is the _____ province in Canada.

6. New Brunswick is _____ than Prince Edward Island.

7. The Atlantic region has a _____ population than the other regions.

E. Writing

Use each word to make a sentence about the Atlantic region.

1. provinces _____

2. farms _____

3. cities _____

4. villages _____

5. rivers _____

6. towns _____

7. lakes _____

8. potatoes _____

Read

Provinces

Quebec
Ontario

Where Is Central Canada?

Central Canada is west of the Atlantic Region and east of the Prairie provinces.

A Look at Central Canada

Central Canada is mostly covered in forest, with many rivers and lakes. Most of Central Canada is covered by a large area of rock called the **Canadian Shield**. Most of the Canadian Shield is covered in forest.

In the **southern** part of Central Canada there are farms, and many cities and towns. Canada's two biggest cities are in the southern part of Central Canada. They are Toronto and Montreal.

There are two provinces in Central Canada.

Quebec is the largest province in Canada. It is mostly covered in forest. There are many farms and large cities in the south. Quebec has a very large river called the St. *Lawrence River*. Quebec City is the capital city of Quebec, but more people live in Montreal. Most people in Quebec speak French.

Ontario is the most populated province in Canada. It is mostly covered in forest, with large cities in the south. It has five very large lakes called the *Great Lakes*.

Compared with the Other Regions of Canada

Central Canada is the most populated region .
Central Canada has the most cities.

Understand What You Read

A. Word Meanings

Write the correct words beside their meanings.

> **Canadian Shield • St. Lawrence River • Great Lakes**
> **Central Canada • Montreal**

1. _____ Ontario and Quebec

2. _____ a large city in Quebec

3. _____ a large area of rock

4. _____ a river in Quebec

5. _____ five large lakes in Ontario

B. Answer the Questions

1. Where is Central Canada?

   _____

2. Name two provinces and capital cities in Central Canada.

   _____

3. Name the capital city of Canada. _____

   What province is it in? _____

4. Name another large city in Quebec. _____

5. What is the Canadian Shield?

   _____

6. What language do most people in Quebec speak? _____

7. Which province is the largest province in Canada? _____

Understand What You Read

C. Circle the Correct Answer

1. Ontario is the
   - smallest
   - most populated
   - largest
   province in Canada.

2. Central Canada is mostly covered in
   - cities
   - forest
   - farms

3. A large river in Quebec is called the
   - Great
   - Atlantic
   - St. Lawrence
   River.

4. The Canadian Shield is
   - rock
   - farmland
   - water

D. Writing

Use each word to make a sentence about Central Canada.

1. largest _____

2. more _____

3. higher _____

4. biggest _____

5. most populated _____

6. French _____

7. west _____

8. two _____

E. Discuss

1. Why do you think this region is called Central Canada?
2. Why do you think Central Canada is the most populated region in Canada?
3. Why do you think so few people live in Northern Ontario or Quebec?

Read

Provinces

Manitoba
Saskatchewan
Alberta

Where Are the Prairie Provinces?

The Prairie provinces are almost in the middle of Canada. There are three provinces in the region.

A Look at the Prairie Provinces

The **northern** half of the Prairie provinces is covered in forest. The **southern** half is mostly flat and has many large farms. The farmers mostly grow wheat and other grains.

Wheat is used to make bread. For this reason, the Prairie provinces are sometimes called **Canada's breadbasket.**

The big cities in the Prairie provinces are Edmonton, Calgary, Winnipeg, Saskatoon and Regina.

What Is the Weather Like?

The Prairie provinces are very cold in the winter. The winters are long and the summers are short. It does not rain very often.

Compared with the Rest of Canada

The Prairie provinces have less rain.
The Prairie provinces have fewer forests.
The Prairie provinces have more farms.

Understand What You Read

A. Word Meanings

Write the correct word beside each meaning. Find the words in the reading.

1. _____ Manitoba, Saskatchewan and Alberta

2. _____ used to make bread

3. _____ capital city of Manitoba

4. _____ capital city of Saskatchewan

5. _____ capital city of Alberta

6. _____ another name for the Prairie provinces

7. _____ a city in Saskatchewan

B. Fill in the Blanks

Write Manitoba, Saskatchewan, Alberta, Winnipeg, Regina and Edmonton on the map.

1. Which Prairie province is next to Ontario? _____

2. Which Prairie province is next to British Columbia? _____

3. What are the Prairie provinces sometimes called? _____

Understand What You Read

C. Circle the Correct Answer

1. The {northern / southern / central} part of the Prairie provinces is covered in forests.

2. The southern part of the Prairie provinces has many {cities / farms / forests}

3. The Prairie provinces have {short / long / rainy} winters.

4. The Prairie provinces have {more / less} rain than other regions.

5. The land in the Prairie provinces is mostly {mountainous / flat}

6. The farmers in the Prairie provinces grow mostly {wheat / potatoes / tomatoes}

D. Writing

Use each word to make a sentence about the Prairie provinces.

1. wheat _____

2. farms _____

3. rain _____

4. flat _____

5. northern _____

6. middle _____

7. southern _____

8. three _____

Read

Provinces

British Columbia

Where Is the West Coast?

The West Coast is Canada's westernmost region. There is only one province in the West Coast region, British Columbia. It is next to the Pacific Ocean.

A Look at the West Coast

Most of British Columbia is covered by the **Rocky Mountains** and forest. Most people in British Columbia live in the southwest part of the province. There is a large city called Vancouver there. Vancouver is Canada's third-biggest city.

The capital city of British Columbia is Victoria. Victoria is on an island called **Vancouver Island**. Vancouver Island is off British Columbia's southwest coast.

What Is the Weather Like?

British Columbia is warmer in the winter than the other regions of Canada. It has mild winters and warm summers.

Compared with the Rest of Canada

The West Coast has more mountains.
The West Coast is warmer than the rest of Canada.

Understand What You Read

A. Word Meanings

Write the correct word beside each meaning. You will find the words in the reading.

1. _____ an ocean on the west side of Canada

2. _____ capital city of British Columbia

3. _____ an island off the southwest coast of British Columbia

4. _____ Canada's third-biggest city

5. _____ mountains in British Columbia

6. _____ British Columbia

B. True or False

Circle T or F. Then write a correct sentence on the line.

1. The West Coast is on the east side of Canada.   T / F

   _____

2. There are two provinces on the West Coast.   T / F

   _____

3. The West Coast is next to the Atlantic Ocean.   T / F

   _____

4. The capital city of British Columbia is Victoria.   T / F

   _____

5. Victoria is on Toronto Island.   T / F

   _____

6. Vancouver is Canada's second-biggest city.   T / F

   _____

Understand What You Read

C. Circle the Correct Answer

1. Vancouver is
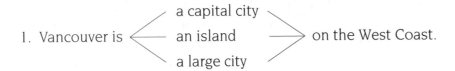
a capital city
an island
a large city
on the West Coast.

2. British Columbia is
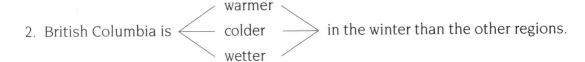
warmer
colder
wetter
in the winter than the other regions.

3. Vancouver is Canada's
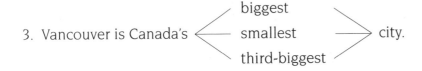
biggest
smallest
third-biggest
city.

4. The West Coast has more
mountains
farms
cities
than the other regions.

5. Most British Columbians live in the
north
southeast
southwest
part of the province.

D. Writing

Use each word to make a sentence about the West Coast.

1. Rocky Mountains _____

2. Victoria _____

3. Vancouver _____

4. warmer _____

5. province _____

6. Pacific Ocean _____

7. forest _____

Read

Territories

Yukon Territory
Northwest Territories

Where Is the North?

The North region is north of Canada's provinces. There are two territories in the North, the Yukon Territory and the Northwest Territories. In 1999 the Northwest Territories will be divided in two. The new territory will be called **Nunavut**. Then there will be three territories in the North.

A Look at the North

The North is the largest region in Canada, but it has the lowest population.

The **Yukon Territory** is west of the Northwest Territories. There are many mountains in the Yukon Territory.

The **Northwest Territories** is the larger territory. It has many islands. The northern-most island is Ellesmere Island. Most of the land in the North is always frozen. There are some forests and a few small cities.

What Is the Weather Like?

It is very cold in the North. The summers are short and the winters are very long.

Compared with the Other Regions of Canada

The North is the biggest region.
The North has the lowest population.
The North is the coldest region.
In the North the winters are longer and the summers are shorter.

Understand What You Read

A. Word Meanings

Write the correct word beside each meaning. You will find the words in the reading.

1. _____ the year the Northwest Territories will be divided in two

2. _____ the name of the new territory

3. _____ an island in the Northwest Territories

4. _____ a territory west of the Northwest Territories

5. _____ the Yukon Territory and the Northwest Territories

B. Circle the Correct Answer

1. The North region is very
   - large
   - small
   - warm

2. Most of the land is always
   - green
   - frozen
   - wet

3. There are many mountains in the
   - Yukon Territory
   - Northwest Territories
   - Prairie provinces

4. The North has the
   - highest
   - lowest
   population in Canada.

5. The Northwest Territories has many
   - capital cities
   - people
   - islands

Understand What You Read

C. Answer the Questions

1. What is the capital city of the Yukon Territory?

   _____

2. What is the capital city of the Northwest Territories?

   _____

3. What will happen to the Northwest Territories in 1999?

   _____

4. What is the northernmost island in the North?

   _____

5. Which ocean is near the North?

   _____

D. Writing

Use each word to make a sentence about the North.

1. territories _____

2. Nunavut _____

3. population _____

4. cold _____

5. mountains _____

6. largest _____

7. winter _____

E. Discuss

1. Why do you think so few people live in the North?
2. Who do you think lives in the North?

Read

The weather is different in each region of Canada.

AVERAGE DAILY TEMPERATURE IN CELSIUS (°C)			
Province or territory	City	In January (°C)	In July (°C)
British Columbia	Vancouver	3	17
Alberta	Edmonton	-15	17
Saskatchewan	Regina	-18	19
Manitoba	Winnipeg	-19	20
Ontario	Toronto	-7	21
Quebec	Montreal	-10	21
Newfoundland	St. John's	-4	16
New Brunswick	St. John	-8	17
Nova Scotia	Halifax	-6	18
Prince Edward Island	Charlottetown	-7	18
Yukon Territory	Whitehorse	-21	14
Northwest Territories	Yellowknife	-29	16

Source: Environment Canada, *Climates of Canada, 1990* (Ottawa: Supply and Services, 1990), various pages.

Temperature tells us how hot or cold something is. In Canada we measure temperature in degrees **Celsius**. The United States measures temperature in degrees Fahrenheit. Canada used to measure temperature in degrees Fahrenheit but changed to Celsius.

Here is a thermometer. It can be used to measure the temperature of the air.

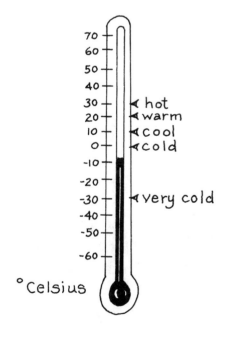

Understand What You Read

A. Fill in the Blanks

Use the words in the box.

cool • warm • hot • cold • very cold

1. It is 10 degrees Celsius. It is _____.

2. It is -10 degrees Celsius. It is _____.

3. It is 20 degrees Celsius. It is _____.

4. It is 30 degrees Celsius. It is _____.

5. It is -25 degrees Celsius. It is _____.

6. It is 18 degrees Celsius. It is _____.

7. It is 40 degrees Celsius. It is _____.

B. Fill in the Blanks

spring • summer • fall • winter

1. It is 15 degrees Celsius. I think it is _____.

2. It is -15 degrees Celsius. I think it is _____.

3. It is 32 degrees Celsius. I think it is _____.

4. It is 12 degrees Celsius. I think it is _____.

C. Discuss

1. What is the temperature today?
2. What is the season today?
3. What season do you like best? Why?
4. When is it warmer, in the morning or in the afternoon? Why?

Understand What You Read

D. Fill in the Blanks

Write the cities from coldest to warmest for January. Write the province or territory and the average temperature beside each city.

	CITY	PROVINCE OR TERRITORY	TEMPERATURE
Coldest	_____	_____	_____
	_____	_____	_____
	_____	_____	_____
	_____	_____	_____
	_____	_____	_____
	_____	_____	_____
	_____	_____	_____
	_____	_____	_____
	_____	_____	_____
	_____	_____	_____
	_____	_____	_____
Warmest	_____	_____	_____

E. Answer the Questions

1. Which two cities are the coldest in January?

   _____

2. Which provinces or territories are these cities in?

   _____

3. What are the next-three-coldest cities?

   _____

4. Which region are these cities in?

   _____

GLOSSARY

Atlantic region:	Nova Scotia, New Brunswick, Prince Edward Island and Newfoundland.
Canada:	The northernmost country in North America.
Canada's breadbasket:	Another name for the Prairie provinces.
Canadian Shield:	A rocky area of land in Canada.
Cape Breton Island:	An island that belongs to Nova Scotia.
Capital city:	The city in which the government is based.
Central Canada:	Ontario and Quebec.
Coast:	Land beside the ocean.
Continent:	A large area of land.
East Coast:	Another name for the Atlantic region.
Ellesmere Island:	An island that belongs to the Northwest Territories.
Great Lakes:	Five large lakes in southern Ontario.
Imperial system:	A system for measuring distance, weight and temperature.
Labrador:	An area of land that belongs to Newfoundland.
Metric system:	A system for measuring distance, weight and temperature.
Montreal:	A city in Quebec.
North (the):	Yukon Territory and the Northwest Territories.
North America:	A continent including Canada, the United States and Mexico.
Nunavut:	Will be the name of a northern territory in 1999.
Population:	The number of people who live in a place.
Prairie provinces:	Manitoba, Saskatchewan and Alberta.
Rocky Mountains:	Mountains in Western Canada.
TransCanada Highway:	A highway that crosses southern Canada.
Vancouver:	A city in British Columbia.
Vancouver Island:	An island that belongs to British Columbia.
Wheat:	A grain used to make bread.

The History

Getting Ready to Learn **44**

UNIT 1   The First Peoples 46

UNIT 2   The Early Settlers 49

UNIT 3   British Rule 52

UNIT 4   Confederation 55

UNIT 5   Settling the West 58

UNIT 6   The Constitution Act 61

UNIT 7   The First Peoples Today 64

UNIT 8   Celebrating Our History 67

Glossary **71**

In Part 2 you will learn about Canada's history. Before you work on the units, answer these questions.

1. Can you find Canada, France and England on the map?

2. Why do you think people from France and England wanted to move to Canada?

3. What do you think Canada was like three hundred years ago?

4. What do you think it was like for people to move to Canada three hundred years ago?

5. How do you think Aboriginal peoples felt when people from France and England came to Canada?

GETTING READY TO LEARN

Think about the topics listed in the left-hand column. In the middle column, write what you already know about the topics. Then write three things you want to find out about the topics in the right-hand column.

ABOUT	I ALREADY KNOW	I WANT TO FIND OUT
First Nations peoples and the Inuit	_____ _____ _____ _____ _____	1. _____ 2. _____ 3. _____
French and British people coming to Canada	_____ _____ _____ _____ _____	1. _____ 2. _____ 3. _____
Canada becoming an independent country	_____ _____ _____ _____ _____	1. _____ 2. _____ 3. _____

Read

The first people to live in Canada were the **Aboriginal peoples**. There are three groups of Aboriginal peoples: the First Nations, the Inuit and the Métis.

Here is a short history of the Aboriginal peoples.

The First Nations

First Nations peoples have lived in Canada for thousands of years. Some people call them *Native peoples*, or *Indians*. They live all over Canada.

Different First Nations **bands** speak different languages. A band is a group of people who have the same customs, language and traditions. There are many First Nations bands.

The Inuit

The Inuit have also lived in Canada for thousands of years. Some people call them *Eskimos* or *Native peoples*.
Most Inuit live in the north of Canada where it is very cold.

Most Inuit speak the same language.

The Métis

In the 1600s some people from Europe came to Canada. First Nations peoples helped them live in Canada. Some people from Europe had children with First Nations people. These children and their families are called *Métis*.

Later, more and more people from Europe came to Canada. They wanted land. The Canadian government decided that some areas of land should be saved for First Nations peoples. The government called these areas of land **reserves**.

Understand What You Read

A. Word Meanings

Write the correct word beside its meaning.

> **Aboriginal • Métis • First Nations • Inuit
> bands • reserves • Eskimos • Indians**

1. _____ a name some people call First Nations peoples

2. _____ groups of people who have the same customs

3. _____ a name some people call the Inuit

4. _____ the first people to live in Canada

5. _____ people who have some First Nations ancestors and some European ancestors

6. _____ areas of land for First Nations peoples

7. _____ an Aboriginal group who live mostly in the north

8. _____ an Aboriginal group who live all over Canada

B. Fill in the Blanks

Use the words above to complete the sentences.

1. There are three groups of _____ peoples in Canada.

2. Canada's Aboriginal peoples are the First Nations, the _____ and the Inuit.

3. The First Nations and the _____ were the first peoples to live in Canada.

4. Some First Nations peoples live on _____.

5. There are many different _____ of First Nations peoples.

Understand What You Read

C. True or False.

Circle T or F. If the sentence is true, copy the sentence on the line. If the sentence is false, write a correct sentence on the line.

1. Reserves are areas of land saved for the Inuit.   T / F

   _____

2. Some people call Inuit peoples Métis.   T / F

   _____

3. First Nations peoples have many languages.   T / F

   _____

4. Most Inuit speak the same language.   T / F

   _____

D. Crossword Puzzle

Across

1. They are sometimes called *Indians*.
2. They are part First Nations, part European.
6. The Inuit live in the _____.

Down

3. They are sometimes called *Eskimos*.
4. People from _____ came to Canada in the 1600s.
5. Some people call the Inuit _____.
7. The _____ peoples were the first people to live in Canada.

Read

The First Nations peoples and the Inuit lived in Canada for thousands of years before other people. When Europeans came to Canada, they wanted to own it. When a country owns land far away, that land is called the country's **colony**.

Both France and England wanted parts of Canada to be their colonies. Some people from France and England came to Canada to live. People who move to a new land are called **settlers.**

French Settlement in the 1500s, 1600s and 1700s

The French government wanted people from France to live in Canada, so France could have Canada as its colony. France sent people to live in Canada to become settlers.

In the 1500s, some French people settled in parts of the Atlantic region. At that time the region was called Acadia, so the settlers were called **Acadians**. They were the first Europeans to settle **permanently** in Canada. Other French people settled in Quebec. The French government called the colonies **New France**.

The French people learned from the First Nations peoples. Some French people had children with First Nations people. Their children were called *Métis*.

By the 1700s, thousands of French settlers lived in New France. Most of them lived in southern Quebec along the St. Lawrence River.

British Settlement in the 1500s, 1600s and 1700s

Many people from England settled in areas of the United States. The British government called these colonies **New England**. There were 13 British colonies in New England.

Understand What You Read

A. Word Meanings

Write the correct word beside its meaning.

Acadians • colony • New England • New France • settlers

1. _____ land a country owns that is far away

2. _____ people who move to a new land to live

3. _____ the first Europeans to settle permanently in Canada

4. _____ British colonies in the United States

5. _____ French colonies in Canada

B. Answer the Questions

1. Which two countries wanted to have colonies in Canada?

   _____

2. Which country sent people to settle in Canada?

   _____

3. What did France call its colonies in Canada?

   _____

4. Where did many British people settle?

   _____

5. What did England call its colonies?

   _____

Understand What You Read

C. Circle the Correct Answer

1. First Nations and Inuit people lived in Canada —— second
   first

2. People from France settled in —— Canada
   the United States

3. People from —— France —— settled in the United States.
   England

4. A —— settler —— is land another country owns.
   colony

5. Acadians were people from —— France
   England

6. People from France settled in the —— west —— of Canada.
   east

7. The Métis are part European and part —— British
   First Nations

8. *Permanent* means a —— short —— time.
   long

D. Discuss

1. Why do you think countries want colonies?
2. How do you think the Aboriginal peoples felt when the Europeans came?
3. Why do you think France and England had colonies on the eastern side of Canada and the United States?

Read

France and England Both Want Canada

France and England both wanted to own parts of Canada in the 1700s. They went to war over who would own Canada.

In 1763 England won the war. The French colonies in Canada became British colonies.

The French and the British

When New France first became British, there were more French people than British people living there. Most French people lived in Quebec.

The French people knew their land was owned by the British government. But they wanted to keep their own language and way of life. The British government agreed. In 1774 the **Quebec Act** was passed. It described how the French people's way of life would be protected.

More British People Come to Canada

Later more and more British people came to Canada. Some people came from England. Others came from Ireland, Scotland and Wales. Other British people came from the United States.

The British people who came from the United States were called **United Empire Loyalists.** They came because the United States became independent from England. But they were still loyal to England. They moved to Canada because Canada was British.

Most of them moved to Ontario and the Atlantic provinces.

Understand What You Read

A. Answer the Questions

1. When did the French colonies become British colonies?

   _____

2. What is a colony?

   _____

3. Why did France and England have a war in Canada?

   _____

4. Where did most French people live?

   _____

5. What did the French people want to keep?

   _____

6. Who were the United Empire Loyalists?

   _____

B. True or False

1. The United Empire Loyalists were loyal to France.   T / F

2. There were more British people than French people in Canada in 1763.   T / F

3. The French people wanted to keep their language.   T / F

4. The United Empire Loyalists came to Canada from the United States.   T / F

5. The Quebec Act was passed in 1763.   T / F

Understand What You Read

C. Fill in the Blanks

war • French • language • France • England

1. Before 1763 parts of Canada were _____ colonies.

2. England and France went to _____ over who would own the colonies.

3. In 1763 _____ won the war.

4. After 1763 _____ did not own the colonies in Canada.

5. After 1763 _____ owned the colonies in Canada.

6. The _____ wanted to keep their _____.

D. Writing

Use each word to write a sentence about British rule.

1. war _____

2. 1763 _____

3. language _____

4. United States _____

5. United Empire Loyalists _____

E. Discuss

1. Why do you think the British government let the French people keep their language?

2. Canada was once a British colony. List some things in Canada today that show this.

3. Canada was once a French colony. List some things in Canada today that show this.

Read

Canadian Leaders Want to Unite the Colonies

In the 1800s more and more people settled in different parts of Canada. Canadian leaders talked about bringing the colonies of Canada together. They wanted to have one government for all of Canada. This government would look after things that concerned the whole country.

But each area in Canada had different concerns. So each area of Canada would have a smaller government of its own. The government of all of Canada would be called the **federal** government. The smaller governments would be called **provincial** governments.

The federal government could look after things for all of Canada, and the provincial governments could look after different things for their own provinces.

The British Government Agrees

The British government agreed to unite the colonies in Canada. The ideas about how to govern Canada were written down. In 1867, the British government made the ideas into law for Canada. The law was called the **British North America Act.** It was called the BNA Act, for short. Canada would set up its own government and follow the ideas in the BNA Act. When a country governs itself, it is **independent**.

On July 1, 1867, **Ontario**, **Quebec**, **Nova Scotia** and **New Brunswick** became the first provinces of the new country, Canada. We call this event **Confederation**. Confederation happens when different areas come together, or unite.

The First Prime Minister

The person who leads the federal government is called the *prime minister*. The first prime minister of Canada was **Sir John A. Macdonald**.

Other Provinces Join Confederation

Later other provinces joined Canada. Manitoba joined three years after Confederation in 1870. British Columbia joined in 1871. Prince Edward Island joined in 1873. Saskatchewan and Alberta joined in 1905. Newfoundland joined last in 1949.

Understand What You Read

A. Word Meanings

Write the correct word beside its meaning.

> **independent • Confederation • BNA Act • federal government**
> **provincial government • prime minister**

1. _____ governs the whole country

2. _____ governs a province

3. _____ leader of the federal government

4. _____ ideas about how to govern Canada

5. _____ when different areas unite

6. _____ when a country governs itself

B. True or False

Circle T or F. Then write a correct sentence on the line.

1. Confederation happens when different areas separate.   T / F

   _____

2. Confederation was in 1967.   T / F

   _____

3. Ontario, Quebec and Alberta became the first provinces of Canada.   T / F

   _____

4. The BNA Act described how the country would be governed.   T / F

   _____

5. Sir David A. Macdonald was the first prime minister of Canada.   T / F

   _____

Understand What You Read

C. Circle the Correct Answer

1. Before 1867 < Britain / France > owned Canada.

2. The federal government is the government of < Canada / a province

3. There were < six / four > Canadian provinces in 1867.

4. The first leader was < Sir John A. Macdonald / Queen Elizabeth

5. The last province to join Canada was < Newfoundland / New Brunswick

D. Fill in the Blanks

Write the year the provinces joined Confederation. Shade the first four provinces of Canada on the map.

Ontario _____

Quebec _____

Nova Scotia _____

New Brunswick _____

Manitoba _____

British Columbia _____

Prince Edward Island _____

Saskatchewan _____

Alberta _____

Newfoundland _____

Read

Canada Builds a Railway

In 1867, only Ontario, Quebec, Nova Scotia and New Brunswick were part of Canada. The Canadian government wanted Canada to reach from the Atlantic Ocean to the Pacific Ocean. So Canada asked British Columbia to join Confederation. British Columbia said it would join only if Canada built a railway.

Why Did British Columbia Want a Railway?

British Columbia was very far from the other provinces. The people in British Columbia felt isolated. *Isolated* means alone or separate from others. The railway would bring the people in British Columbia the things they needed to live.

Canada agreed to build the railway. The railway was finished in 1885.

Canada Wants More People

Canada had a lot of land and a railway, but it needed more people. Canada needed people to farm the land.

Canada promised people free land in Western Canada. Many people accepted the land and moved to Western Canada. Between 1901 and 1911 Canada grew by almost two million people!

First Nations and Métis

The First Nations and Métis peoples already lived in the West. They were upset Canada was giving away land they lived on. The government set up reserves for the First Nations peoples, but they didn't like this. They wanted things to stay the same.

Understand What You Read

A. Answer the Questions

1. Why did Canada build the railway?

   _____

2. Why did British Columbia join Canada?

   _____

3. Why did the people in British Columbia want a railway?

   _____

4. Why did Canada need more people?

   _____

5. Why did people move to Western Canada?

   _____

6. Why were the First Nations and Métis peoples upset?

   _____

B. True or False

Circle T or F.

1. Ontario, Quebec and Alberta were the first provinces to join Canada.   T / F

2. The people in British Columbia wanted a railway.   T / F

3. Canada promised people free land.   T / F

4. Between 1901 and 1911 Canada grew by eight million people.   T / F

5. Reserves are areas of land saved for First Nations peoples.   T / F

Understand What You Read

C. Match

Match the columns to make sentences.

A. The Canadian government   _____ felt isolated.

B. British Columbia   _____ was the last province to join Canada.

C. Newfoundland   _____ asked Canada to build a railway.

D. Ontario   _____ wanted more people in Canada.

E. The people in British Columbia   _____ joined Confederation in 1867.

Copy the Sentences

1. _____

2. _____

3. _____

4. _____

5. _____

D. Discuss

1. Do you think a railway could help a country grow? How?
2. Would you move to a new country if the government gave you free land?
   Discuss the advantages and disadvantages of becoming a settler.
3. Why do you think the Métis and the First Nations peoples were upset?
   Why do you think they did not like the reserves?

Read

Canada Wants to Be More Independent

Before 1867 Canada was a British colony. In 1867 the British government let Canada govern itself. When a country governs itself, it is independent.

After 1867 the British government still had some power in Canada. Canada could not change the rules of the country, the BNA Act, without permission from the British government.

As time passed, Canadians wanted to be more independent.

Canada Becomes More Independent

In 1982 Canadian leaders looked at the ideas in the BNA Act again. They decided to make some important changes. Three important changes were the following:

1. They changed the name of the BNA Act to the **Constitution Act.** The Constitution Act lists the most important rules of Canada.

2. Freedom and equal treatment for all people were important to Canadians. So Canadian leaders wrote a list of things Canadians should have the freedom to do. The list was called the **Charter of Rights and Freedoms**. The leaders added it to the Constitution.

3. Canadian leaders also decided that Canada should be able to change the Constitution Act without asking the British government.

The British government agreed with all the changes. Canada's prime minister and the Queen of England signed their names. This made the changes legal.

Understand What You Read

A. Fill in the Blanks

Constitution Act • 1982 • 1867 • Queen of England
prime minister • BNA Act • rules

1. The Constitution Act is a list of the most important _____ of Canada.

2. The short form of the British North America Act is the _____.

3. The British government passed the BNA Act in _____.

4. Canadian leaders made some changes to the BNA Act in _____.

5. Canadian leaders changed the name of the BNA Act to the _____.

6. The _____ _____ and the _____ _____

   _____ signed the Constitution Act to make the changes legal.

B. Answer the Questions

1. In 1982 Canadian leaders changed the BNA Act. List three important changes:

   a) _____

   _____

   b) _____

   _____

   c) _____

   _____

2. What is the Charter of Rights and Freedoms?

   _____

   _____

Understand What You Read

C. Circle the Correct Answer

1. Before 1867 Canada was _____.

    a) a French colony

    b) an independent country

    c) a British colony

2. On July 1, 1867, Canada became _____.

    a) an independent country

    b) a French colony

    c) a British colony

3. The BNA Act described _____.

    a) how Canada would be governed

    b) what to eat

    c) the Charter of Rights and Freedoms

4. The Constitution Act is the new name for _____.

    a) the Charter of Rights and Freedoms

    b) the BNA Act

    c) Canada

5. In _____ Canadian leaders made some changes to the BNA Act.

    a) 1867

    b) 1870

    c) 1982

6. The Charter of Rights and Freedoms tells about _____.

    a) the things all Canadians have freedom to do

    b) the things everyone in the world has freedom to do

    c) the things all British people have freedom to do

D. Discuss

1. What do you think some of our rights are?

2. What can we do if our rights are not being respected?

Read

There are about 30 million people living in Canada today. About one million are Aboriginal peoples.

Today, Aboriginal peoples are trying to keep their languages and their ways of life. Some Aboriginal groups want their own governments.

First Nations Peoples Today

About eight hundred thousand First Nations peoples live in Canada. There are many different bands of First Nations peoples. Most bands have their own language. They live in all parts of Canada. Some First Nations peoples live on reserves. Others live in cities and towns.

The Inuit Today

About fifty thousand Inuit live in Canada. Most Inuit peoples live in the Northwest Territories. In 1999 a part of the Northwest Territories will be governed by the Inuit. It will be called *Nunavut*.

The Métis Today

About two hundred thousand Métis live in Canada. Most Métis people live in the Prairie provinces.

Understand What You Read

A. Answer the Questions

1. Who are Aboriginal peoples?

   _____

2. About how many people live in Canada today?

   _____

3. Where do some First Nations peoples live?

   _____

4. Where do most Inuit live?

   _____

5. Where do many Métis live?

   _____

B. Fill in the Blanks

> **Métis • First Nations • Aboriginal • Inuit**
> **Nunavut • reserves**

1. Most Aboriginal peoples in Canada are _____ peoples.

2. There are about one million _____ peoples in Canada.

3. Most _____ peoples live in the Northwest Territories.

4. The Inuit will govern an area of land called _____.

5. Most _____ live in the Prairie provinces.

6. Some First Nations peoples live on _____.

Understand What You Read

C. Sort

Write the words under *First Nations*, *Inuit* or *Métis*. One word will be used three times.

> **Northwest Territories • Prairie provinces • Aboriginal
> two hundred thousand • eight hundred thousand • fifty thousand
> Nunavut • reserves**

FIRST NATIONS	INUIT	MÉTIS
_____	_____	_____
_____	_____	_____
_____	_____	_____
	_____	

D. Writing

Use the word or number to write a sentence about Aboriginal peoples.

1. reserves _____

2. one million _____

3. eight hundred thousand _____

4. Nunavut _____

5. Northwest Territories _____

6. fifty thousand _____

7. 30 million _____

8. Prairie provinces _____

9. two hundred thousand _____

Read

Canadians remember and celebrate their history every year.

Victoria Day

Canadians remember that Canada was a British colony. Every year many Canadians celebrate Queen Victoria's birthday. She was born on May 24, 1819. She was the Queen of England when Canada became a country in 1867. So every year, the third Monday in May is a holiday. We call this holiday **Victoria Day**.

Today the queen is Queen Elizabeth II.

The Queen's Role Today

Canada also remembers and respects England by keeping the Queen of England as the head of government.

The Queen's picture is on all of our coins and on some of our stamps.

Understand What You Read

A. Answer the Questions

1. Who was the Queen of England in 1867?

   _____

2. What is the queen's name today?

   _____

3. What do Canadians celebrate on the third Monday in May?

   _____

4. What is the Queen's role in Canada?

   _____

B. Circle the Correct Answer

1. The Queen's picture is on all of Canada's
   - bills
   - coins

2. Victoria Day celebrates Queen Victoria's
   - birthday
   - marriage

3. Today the queen's name is
   - Queen Elizabeth II
   - Queen Victoria

4. Canadians remember that Canada was
   - a British colony
   - an American colony

Read

Before 1763 Canada was a French colony. Then in 1763 Canada became a British colony. Finally in 1867 Canada became a country and set up its own government. Every year Canada celebrates the day it became independent.

Canada Day

Canada became independent on July 1, 1867. So every year on July 1st we celebrate Canada's birthday. This holiday is called **Canada Day.**

Canada's First Prime Minister

The prime minister when Canada became independent was Sir John A. Macdonald. His picture is on our 10-dollar bill.

Understand What You Read

C. Match

Match the words to make sentences.

A. Canada Day   _____ Canada was a French colony.

B. In 1763   _____ is on the third Monday in May.

C. Before 1763   _____ is on July 1st.

D. On July 1, 1867   _____ was the first prime minister.

E. Victoria Day   _____ Canada became a British colony.

F. Sir John A. Macdonald   _____ Canada became independent.

Copy the sentences above.

1. _____

2. _____

3. _____

4. _____

5. _____

6. _____

D. Answer the Questions

1. How old is Canada? _____

2. What year was Canada one-year-old? _____

3. Who governed Canada before 1867? _____

GLOSSARY

Aboriginal peoples:	The first people to live in Canada.
Acadia:	The name of parts of the Atlantic region in the 1600s.
Acadians:	The people from France who settled in Acadia.
Band:	A group of Aboriginal people who have the same customs.
BNA Act:	A document signed by the British government in 1867. It explained how Canada would be governed.
Canada Day:	A holiday on July 1st celebrating Canada's birthday.
Charter of Rights and Freedoms:	A list of things all Canadians have the freedom to do.
Colony:	Land a country owns that is far away.
Confederation:	The union of different areas of land.
Constitution Act:	The new name given to the BNA Act in 1982.
Eskimo:	A name some people call the Inuit.
First Nations:	A group of Aboriginal peoples.
Independent:	When a country governs itself.
Inuit:	A group of Aboriginal peoples who live in the North.
Isolated:	Feeling alone and separate from others.
Métis:	People descended from First Nations and European people.
New England:	British colonies in what is now the United States.
New France:	French colonies in what is now Canada.
Nunavut:	Will be the name of a northern territory in 1999.
Quebec Act:	Described how French people in Canada could keep their language.
Reserves:	Areas of land saved for First Nations peoples.
Settlers:	People who move to a new land.
United Empire Loyalists:	People who moved from the United States to Canada after the United States became independent.
Victoria Day:	A holiday on the third Monday in May celebrating Queen Victoria's birthday.

PART 3

The People

Getting Ready to Learn **74**

UNIT 1   The Population of Canada 75

UNIT 2   The Populations of Other Countries 79

UNIT 3   Where Canadians Live 81

UNIT 4   Who Canadians Are 84

UNIT 5   Immigration 87

UNIT 6   Languages Canadians Speak 90

UNIT 7   Canadians and Work 93

UNIT 8   Canadians Help Each Other 97

Glossary **100**

Think about the topics listed in the left-hand column. In the middle column, write what you already know about the topics. Then write three things you want to find out about the topics in the right-hand column.

ABOUT	I ALREADY KNOW	I WANT TO FIND OUT
Canada's population	_____ _____ _____ _____ _____	1. _____ 2. _____ 3. _____
the number of immigrants in Canada	_____ _____ _____ _____ _____	1. _____ 2. _____ 3. _____
jobs in Canada	_____ _____ _____ _____ _____	1. _____ 2. _____ 3. _____

Answer the Questions

1. Where do you think most people in Canada live?

2. Do you think Canada needs more people?

3. Why do you think people immigrate to Canada?

Read

Canada is a very big country. It is the second-biggest country in the world. But it does not have a big **population** compared with other countries of its size. The population of a country or a city is the number of people who live there.

How Many People Live in Canada?

Canada's population is about 30 million people.

Where Do People in Canada Live?

Most people in Canada live in the southern part of the country, along the shaded part of the map. They live in cities and towns. Toronto, Montreal and Vancouver have the highest populations. Very few people live in the northern part of the country.

How Do We Know Where People Live?

Every five years the government counts the people who live in Canada. This is called a **census**. There was a census in 1996. Here are the population numbers from the 1996 census.

PROVINCE OR TERRITORY	1996 POPULATION
British Columbia	3 724 500
Alberta	2 696 826
Saskatchewan	990 237
Manitoba	1 113 898
Ontario	10 753 573
Quebec	7 138 795
Newfoundland	551 792
New Brunswick	738 113
Nova Scotia	909 282
Prince Edward Island	134 557
Yukon Territory	30 766
Northwest Territories	64 402
Total	**28 846 761**

Source: Statistics Canada, *A National Overview*, 1997, Catalogue No. 93-357-XPB, page 11.

Understand What You Read

A. Fill in the Blanks

Write the provinces and territories and their populations, from the highest to the lowest population.

	PROVINCE OR TERRITORY	POPULATION
Highest population	_____	_____
	_____	_____
	_____	_____
	_____	_____
	_____	_____
	_____	_____
	_____	_____
	_____	_____
	_____	_____
	_____	_____
	_____	_____
	_____	_____
Lowest population	_____	_____

B. Answer the Questions

1. Which province had the highest population in 1996? _____

2. Which province had the second-highest population? _____

3. Which province had the third-highest population? _____

4. Which three cities have the highest populations?

    _____

5. Which three provinces are these cities in?

    _____

Read

<table>
<tr><td colspan="4" align="center">CENSUS RESULTS FOR 1991 AND 1996</td></tr>
<tr><td></td><td align="center">Population
1991</td><td align="center">Population
1996</td><td align="center">Population
for this year</td></tr>
<tr><td>Canada</td><td>27 296 859</td><td>28 846 761</td><td>_____</td></tr>
<tr><td>British Columbia</td><td>3 282 061</td><td>3 724 500</td><td>_____</td></tr>
<tr><td>Alberta</td><td>2 545 553</td><td>2 696 826</td><td>_____</td></tr>
<tr><td>Saskatchewan</td><td>988 928</td><td>990 237</td><td>_____</td></tr>
<tr><td>Manitoba</td><td>1 091 942</td><td>1 113 898</td><td>_____</td></tr>
<tr><td>Ontario</td><td>10 084 885</td><td>10 753 573</td><td>_____</td></tr>
<tr><td>Quebec</td><td>6 895 963</td><td>7 138 795</td><td>_____</td></tr>
<tr><td>New Brunswick</td><td>723 900</td><td>738 133</td><td>_____</td></tr>
<tr><td>Nova Scotia</td><td>899 942</td><td>909 282</td><td>_____</td></tr>
<tr><td>Prince Edward Island</td><td>129 765</td><td>134 557</td><td>_____</td></tr>
<tr><td>Newfoundland</td><td>568 474</td><td>551 792</td><td>_____</td></tr>
<tr><td>Yukon Territory</td><td>27 797</td><td>30 766</td><td>_____</td></tr>
<tr><td>Northwest Territories</td><td>57 649</td><td>64 402</td><td>_____</td></tr>
</table>

Source: Statistics Canada, *A National Overview*, 1997, Catalogue No. 93-357-XPB, page 11.

You can find out Canada's population for this year by phoning **Statistics Canada.**

<table>
<tr><td colspan="3" align="center">PHONE NUMBERS FOR STATISTICS CANADA</td></tr>
<tr><td>Province or territory</td><td>Toll-free number</td><td>City</td></tr>
<tr><td>British Columbia
Yukon Territory</td><td>1-800-663-1551</td><td>Vancouver . . . . .666-3691</td></tr>
<tr><td>Saskatchewan . . . .</td><td>1-800-667-7164</td><td>Regina . . . . .780-5405</td></tr>
<tr><td>Manitoba . . . .</td><td>1-800-661-7828</td><td>Winnipeg . . . . .983-4020</td></tr>
<tr><td>Alberta
Northwest Territories</td><td>1-800-563-7828</td><td>Edmonton 495-3027
Calgary . . . . .292-6717</td></tr>
<tr><td>Ontario . . . .</td><td>1-800-263-1136</td><td>Toronto. 973-6586
Ottawa . . . . .951-8116</td></tr>
<tr><td>Quebec . . . .</td><td>1-800-361-2831</td><td>Montreal . . . . .283-5725</td></tr>
<tr><td>Newfoundland
Nova Scotia
New Brunswick
Prince Edward Island</td><td>1-800-565-7192</td><td>Halifax . . . . .426-5331</td></tr>
</table>

Source: Statistics Canada.

Understand What You Read

C. Fill in the Blanks

1. Canada's population in 1991 was _____.

2. Canada's population in 1996 was _____.

3. There is a census every _____ years.

4. There was a census in 1991 and a census in 1996. The next census will be in _____.

D. Answer the Questions

1. Did the population of every province increase, or get bigger, from 1991 to 1996?

   _____

2. Which province had a decrease in population?

   _____

3. How many more people lived in Canada in 1996 than in 1991?

   _____

   Phone Statistics Canada. Find out what the populations are for this year. Write the numbers on page 77.

4. What is the Statistics Canada toll-free phone number for your province?

   _____

E. Discuss

1. Do you think Canada's population will keep increasing?
2. Do you think it is good for Canada to have a higher population? Why?

Read

Canada is the second-biggest country in the world. But Canada does not have a very high population compared with many countries. Here are the 10 countries that have the highest populations.

Canada's population is about 30 million.

THE 10 MOST POPULATED COUNTRIES	
1. China	1 209 110 000
2. India	944 980 000
3. United States	265 130 000
4. Indonesia	196 830 000
5. Brazil	161 700 000
6. Russia	150 500 000
7. Japan	125 760 000
8. Pakistan	132 330 000
9. Bangladesh	129 500 000
10. Nigeria	108 850 000

Find the 10 countries on the map.

Understand What You Read

A. Answer the Questions

1. Which country has the highest population? _____

2. Which country has the second-highest population? _____

3. Which country has the third-highest population? _____

4. Which country looks the smallest on the map? _____

5. What is the population of Bangladesh? _____

6. Is Canada bigger than Bangladesh? _____

7. What is the population of Canada? _____

8. Which country has a higher population, Canada or Bangladesh? _____

B. Crossword Puzzle

Across

1. The _____ _____ is south of Canada
3. _____ is the number of people living in a place
5. _____ is a big country with a low population
6. _____ has a population of 132 330 000

Down

2. _____ is a country with many islands
4. _____ is a small country with a high population
5. _____ has the highest population in the world

Read

North or South

Most Canadians live in the southern part of Canada. The northern part of Canada is very cold. It is mostly covered in forest.

Urban or Rural

An **urban** area is an area that has many houses, stores, roads, restaurants and buildings. A city or a town is an urban area.

A **rural** area is a small village or a farming area.

Most people in Canada live in urban areas. There are many rural areas in Canada, but the **majority** of people live in cities and towns. *Majority* means more than half. **Minority** means less than half.

RURAL AND URBAN POPULATIONS IN 1996		
Province or territory	**Rural**	**Urban**
British Columbia	667 112	3 057 388
Alberta	554 011	2 142 815
Saskatchewan	363 059	627 178
Manitoba	313 835	800 063
Ontario	1 794 832	8 958 741
Quebec	1 541 170	5 597 625
Newfoundland	237 973	313 819
New Brunswick	377 712	360 421
Nova Scotia	411 424	497 858
Prince Edward Island	75 097	59 460
Yukon Territory	12 319	18 447
Northwest Territories	37 007	27 395
Total	**6 385 551**	**22 461 210**

Source: Statistics Canada, *A National Overview*, 1997, Catalogue No. 93-357-XPB, from 1996 Census Data, page 183.

Understand What You Read

A. Word Meanings

majority • minority • census • population

1. _____ more than half

2. _____ less than half

3. _____ a population count

4. _____ the number of people who live in a place

B. Circle the Correct Answer

1. Most Canadians live in the _____ part of Canada.

   a) northern

   b) middle

   c) southern

2. An example of an urban area is _____.

   a) a farm

   b) a city

   c) a small town

3. A majority is _____.

   a) about half

   b) more than half

   c) less than half

4. The majority of Canadians live in _____.

   a) urban areas

   b) rural areas

   c) small towns

Understand What You Read

C. Answer the Questions

1. Look at the populations of each province on page 81. Put a check mark (✔) under *Majority Rural* or *Majority Urban*.

PROVINCE OR TERRITORY	MAJORITY RURAL	MAJORITY URBAN
British Columbia		
Alberta		
Saskatchewan		
Manitoba		
Ontario		
Quebec		
Newfoundland		
New Brunswick		
Nova Scotia		
Prince Edward Island		
Yukon Territory		
Northwest Territories		

2. Which provinces or territories have a majority of people living in rural areas?

D. Discuss

1. Why do you think most Canadians live in the southern part of the country?
2. Why do you think most Canadians live in urban areas?
3. Do you prefer to live in an urban area or a rural area? Why?

Read

There are about 30 million people in Canada. Some of these people's **ancestors** lived in Canada a long time ago. But most of these people's ancestors lived in other countries. All these people, no matter where they are from, are Canadians.

An **ancestor** is a relative from a long time ago, like a grandparent or a great-grandparent.

Who Are Canadians?

Canadians are
Aboriginal peoples
people with French and British ancestors
people from many countries
people with ancestors from many countries

Aboriginal Peoples

Aboriginal peoples were the first people to live in Canada. There are about one million Aboriginal peoples living in Canada today.

People with British and French Ancestors

The largest group of people in Canada have British or French ancestors. The French and the British people were the first Europeans to settle in Canada. This is why so many Canadians have French or British ancestors.

People from Other Countries

Many people in Canada were born in other countries. These people are **immigrants.** There are about four million immigrants in Canada. Many other people were born in Canada but have ancestors from countries such as Germany, Italy, China, Ukraine, Jamaica and India.

Understand What You Read

A. Word Meanings

Write the correct word beside its meaning.

ancestor • immigrant • Aboriginal peoples

1. _____ First Nations peoples, Inuit and Métis

2. _____ a person who was born in one country, then moved to another country to live

3. _____ a parent, grandparent or great-grandparent

B. Crossword Puzzle

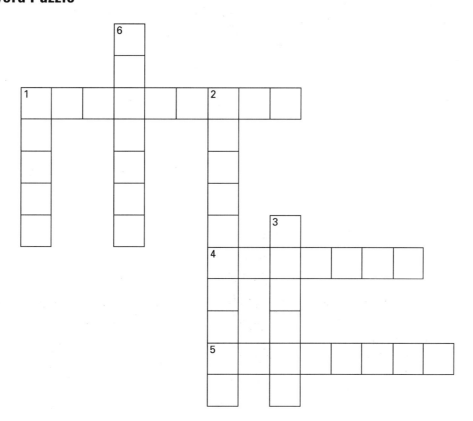

Across

1. Someone who moved to Canada from another country
4. Many Canadians have ancestors from _____
5. My great-grandfather is my _____

Down

1. Many Canadians have ancestors from _____
2. _____ peoples were the first people in Canada
3. Many Canadians have <u>F</u>_____ ancestors
6. Many Canadians have <u>B</u>_____ ancestors

Understand What You Read

C. Writing

Use the word to make a sentence about people in Canada.

1. 30 million _____

2. one million _____

3. four million _____

4. immigrant _____

5. ancestor _____

D. Fill in the Blanks

Use information from your own life to complete the sentences.

1. I was born in _____.

2. My mother was born in _____.

3. My father was born in _____.

4. My ancestors are from _____.

5. The first language I learned was _____.

Use information about a friend to complete the sentences.

1. _____ was born in _____.

2. _____ mother was born in _____.

3. _____ father was born in _____.

4. _____ has ancestors from _____.

5. The first language _____ learned was _____.

UNIT 5—Immigration

Read

What Is Immigration?

Every year many people from other countries immigrate to Canada. **To immigrate** to a country is to move to that country to live. An immigrant is a person who was born in one country, then moves to another country to live.

In 1995, 209 398 people immigrated to Canada. They came from all over the world.

Where Did These People Come From?

IMMIGRANTS TO CANADA IN 1995	
Continent or region	Number
Asia	126 982
Europe	40 735
North and Central America	18 289
Africa	14 010
South America	7 574
Australasia	1 034
Oceania and other Ocean Islands	774
Total	**209 398**

Source: Statistics Canada, *Annual Demographic Statistics*, Catalogue No. 91-213, page 239.

How Many Immigrants Are There in Canada?

Every year people immigrate to Canada. The 1991 census showed that about four million immigrants live in Canada. Remember, there are about 30 million people in Canada.

Understand What You Read

A. Answer the Questions

1. How many people immigrated to Canada in 1995? _____

2. Do people immigrate to Canada every year? _____

3. About how many immigrants live in Canada now? _____

4. John's parents immigrated to Canada before he was born.
   Is John an immigrant? Why?

   _____

B. Fill in the Blanks

Write the correct numbers on the lines to show how many people from each part of the world immigrated to Canada in 1995.

126 982 • 40 735 • 18 289 • 14 010 • 7 574 • 1 034

Understand What You Read

C. Circle the Correct Answer

1. In 1995 most immigrants came from _____.

   a) Asia

   b) Europe

   c) South America

2. The majority of immigrants came from _____ in 1995.

   a) South America

   b) Africa

   c) Asia

3. The majority of Canadians _____ .

   a) are from Asia

   b) are immigrants

   c) are not immigrants

4. About forty thousand people immigrated to Canada from _____ in 1995.

   a) Asia

   b) Africa

   c) Europe

D. True or False
Circle T or F.

1. There are about two hundred thousand immigrants living in Canada.   T / F

2. About two hundred thousand people immigrated to Canada in 1995.   T / F

3. The majority of Canadians are immigrants.   T / F

4. A person who was born in Canada is an immigrant.   T / F

E. Discuss

1. Why do you think people immigrate to Canada?

2. List three difficult things about immigrating to Canada.

3. Do you have ancestors who immigrated to Canada?

Read

What Are Canada's Official Languages?

An **official language** is a language the government uses. Canada has two official languages, English and French. The first Europeans to live in Canada were French and British, so the government decided that Canada would be **bilingual.** *Bilingual* means that a country or a person has two languages. A bilingual person can speak two languages. A bilingual country has two official languages.

Because Canada is bilingual, Canadians can get information and service from the government of Canada in English or French. All products sold in Canada must have French and English writing on the package.

Other Languages in Canada

Many Canadians speak languages other than English or French. The first language a person learns and still understands is called his or her **mother tongue**.

THE 13 MOST COMMON MOTHER-TONGUE LANGUAGES IN CANADA	
Language	**Number of Speakers**
English	about 16 500 000
French	about 6 500 000
Italian	512 005
Chinese	492 400
German	475 710
Portuguese	211 040
Polish	196 895
Ukrainian	196 160
Aboriginal languages	192 765
Spanish	186 255
Dutch	138 755
Punjabi	134 685
Greek	129 685

Source: Statistics Canada, *1991 Census Highlights–The Daily*, Catalogue No. 96-304, page 29.

Understand What You Read

A. Answer the Questions

1. What is a mother tongue?

   _____

2. What is an official language?

   _____

3. What are the two official languages in Canada?

   _____

4. What does *bilingual* mean?

   _____

5. Why did the government decide to make Canada bilingual?

   _____

B. Circle the Correct Answer

1. A bilingual person can speak _____.

   a) three languages

   b) one language

   c) two languages

2. An official language is a language that _____.

   a) the government uses

   b) every person speaks

   c) is a mother tongue

3. A mother tongue is _____.

   a) the tongue of a mother

   b) the first language a person learns and still understands

   c) the language your mother speaks

Understand What You Read

C. True or False

Circle T or F. Then write a correct sentence on the line. If the sentence is true, copy the sentence.

1. Most Canadians speak Italian.   T / F

   _____

2. The majority of Canadians speak English.   T / F

   _____

3. About five hundred thousand people in Canada can understand Italian.   T / F

   _____

4. The four languages Canadians most commonly understand are English,
   French, Polish and Greek.   T / F

   _____

5. More people can understand Chinese than Italian.   T / F

   _____

6. More people can understand Polish than German.   T / F

   _____

7. There is French and English writing on a milk carton.   T / F

   _____

8. English and Italian are the two official languages in Canada.   T / F

   _____

D. Discuss

1. Are you bilingual?
2. What is your mother tongue?
3. Do you think Canada should have more than two official languages? Why?

Read

Canadians work at many different jobs. Most jobs are in the service industry, trade industry or manufacturing industry. Some Canadians work in the primary industry.

Primary Industry

Some people catch fish, trap animals, cut down trees, work in mines or work on farms. These people work in the **primary industry.** Primary industry workers take things from nature that we can use. These things are called **natural resources.**

Manufacturing Industry

Many people work in factories. These people work in the **manufacturing industry.** Natural resources like trees, fish or copper are sold to factories. Manufacturing jobs use these things to make the goods we buy and use every day, such as paper, food, furniture and tools.

Trade Industry

Many people buy goods that are made in the manufacturing industries and sell them to stores. Others work in stores to sell the goods. These people work in the **trade industry**.

Service Industry

Many people work in restaurants, hair salons, travel agencies, banks, offices, hotels, hospitals or dry cleaners. These people work in the **service industry.** Service industry jobs provide people with things they want or need.

Understand What You Read

A. Circle the Correct Answer

1. Primary industry workers
   - take things from nature
   - make things in factories

2. Manufacturing industry jobs
   - take things from nature
   - make things in factories

3. Natural resources are
   - things in nature we can use
   - things we make in factories

4. Some natural resources are
   - paper, furniture and tools
   - trees, fish and copper

5. Service industry jobs
   - provide people with things they want
   - buy and sell things

B. Fill in the Blanks

Write the correct industry under each picture.

primary industry • manufacturing industry • trade industry • service industry

_____

_____

_____

_____

Understand What You Read

C. Sort

Write the words under *Primary, Trade, Service* or *Manufacturing*.

> **lumberjack • waiter • storeowner • hair stylist • factory worker
> fisherman • bank teller • miner • furniture maker
> wholesaler • distributor**

Primary Industry

_____

_____

_____

Manufacturing Industry

_____

_____

Trade Industry

_____

_____

Service Industry

_____

_____

D. Discuss

1. What industry do you work in?
2. What industry would you like to work in?
3. Where do you think most primary industry jobs are?
4. Where do you think most service industry jobs are?

Understand What You Read

Most Canadians work for an hourly wage. The **minimum wage** is the lowest hourly wage an employer can pay you. An employer can pay you more, but he or she cannot pay you less than the minimum wage. Here is the minimum wage for each province.

MINIMUM WAGES IN DOLLARS PER HOUR FOR 1997	
Province or territory	**Hourly wage ($)**
British Columbia	7.00
Alberta	5.00
Saskatchewan	5.60
Manitoba	5.40
Ontario	6.85
Quebec	6.70
Newfoundland	5.25
New Brunswick	5.50
Nova Scotia	5.50
Prince Edward Island	5.40
Yukon Territory	6.86
Northwest Territories	6.50

Source: Human Resources Development Canada, Workplace Information Directorate.

E. Answer the Questions

1. Which two provinces have the highest minimum wage?

_____

2. Which two provinces have the lowest minimum wage?

_____

3. What does *minimum wage* mean?

_____

F. Discuss

1. Do you think some employers pay less than minimum wage?
2. Why do you think some provinces have a higher minimum wage than other provinces?

Read

Most people in Canada have jobs, but some do not. Some people are able to work but they cannot find jobs. They are **unemployed.**

The Canadian government helps people who do not have jobs by giving them unemployment insurance or social assistance. People who do not work anymore because of their age get **pensions**.

Unemployment Insurance

When Canadians get laid off from their jobs, the government gives them some of their salary for a few months. This is called *unemployment insurance*. It is called UI for short.

Social Assistance

When Canadians cannot find jobs or cannot work, the government gives them some money every month to live on. This is called *social assistance*.

Pension

When Canadians turn sixty-five, the government gives them some money every month. This is called a *pension*.

How Does the Government Get Money to Help Canadians?

Canadians give money to the government. We pay **taxes** on things we buy and on money we make at jobs. These taxes go to the government. The government uses tax money to pay for services Canadians need.

Statement of Earnings and Deductions

Earnings	$1500.00
Federal tax	250.00
Other deductions	200.00
Net pay	$1050.00

Understand What You Read

A. True or False

Circle T or F. If the sentence is true, copy the sentence. If it is false, write a correct sentence.

1. Most people in Canada do not have jobs.   T / F

   _____

2. The government gives UI to people who are sixty-five and over.   T / F

   _____

3. The government gives pensions to people who get laid off.   T / F

   _____

4. The government gives social assistance to people who cannot find jobs. T / F

   _____

5. The government gets money from taxes to help people.   T / F

   _____

B. Circle the Correct Answer

1. Joe is seventy-eight. Every month he gets money from the government.

   Joe receives _____.   a) social assistance

                                           b) a pension

                                           c) unemployment insurance

2. Bill got laid off from his job. Every month he gets some money from the government.

   Bill receives _____.   a) social assistance

                                           b) unemployment insurance

                                           c) a pension

3. Sam cannot find a job. Every month he gets some money from the government.

   Sam receives _____.   a) unemployment insurance

                                           b) a pension

                                           c) social assistance

Understand What You Read

Here is the unemployment rate for each province.

PROVINCIAL UNEMPLOYMENT RATES FOR JULY 1996	
Province	**Unemployment rates**
Newfoundland	18.6 (for every 100 people, 18.6 are unemployed)
Prince Edward Island	14.5 (for every 100 people, 14.5 are unemployed)
Nova Scotia	12.2
New Brunswick	11.4
Quebec	12.4
Ontario	9.2
Manitoba	8.1
Saskatchewan	7.0
Alberta	6.8
British Columbia	8.1

Source: Statistics Canada, *The Labour Force*, Catalogue No. 71-001, page B-3.

C. Answer the Questions

1. For every one hundred people in Ontario, how many were unemployed in July 1996?

   _____

2. Which province had the highest unemployment rate in July 1996? _____

3. Which three provinces had the highest unemployment rates?

   _____

4. Which three provinces had the lowest unemployment rates?

   _____

5. Which region are these provinces in? _____

6. Is it better to have a high unemployment rate or a low unemployment rate?

   _____

   _____

GLOSSARY

Ancestor:	A relative from a long time ago, like a great-grandparent.
Bilingual:	Having two languages.
Census:	An official count of the population.
Immigrant:	Someone who was born in one country, then moves to another country to live.
Immigrate:	To move to another country.
Majority:	More than half.
Manufacturing industry:	Workers who make things in factories.
Minority:	Less than half.
Mother tongue:	The first language a person learns.
Natural resources:	Things we find in nature that we can use.
Official language:	The language the government uses.
Pension:	Money paid regularly to a person after he or she retires.
Population:	The number of people living in a place.
Primary industry:	Workers who take things from nature.
Rural:	A small village or farming area.
Service industry:	Workers who serve people things they want or need.
Social assistance:	Money paid to a person who cannot find a job or cannot work.
Statistics Canada:	Offers information on the results of the census.
Taxes:	Money we pay the government.
Toll-free:	A free long-distance phone call.
Trade industry:	The buying and selling of things.
Unemployed:	Not having a job.
Unemployment insurance:	Money paid to a person laid off from his or her job.
Unemployment rate:	The number of unemployed people for every one hundred people.
Urban:	An area with many houses, stores, roads and buildings.

PART 4
The Government

Getting Ready to Learn **103**

UNIT 1   The Levels of Government 104

UNIT 2   Canada Is a Democracy 108

UNIT 3   An Election 111

UNIT 4   How We Vote 113

The Federal Government **116**

UNIT 5   Ridings 116

UNIT 6   Members of Parliament 119

UNIT 7   House of Commons 121

UNIT 8   Political Parties 123

UNIT 9   The Prime Minister 125

UNIT 10 Prime Ministers of Canada 129

UNIT 11 The Cabinet 131

UNIT 12 The Senate 134

UNIT 13 The Governor General 136

UNIT 14 Summary 138

The Provincial Government **139**

UNIT 15 Ridings 139

UNIT 16 Members of the Provincial Government 142

Elections Office Phone Numbers 146

UNIT 17 Political Parties 147

UNIT 18 The Premier 148

UNIT 19 The Cabinet 151

UNIT 20 The Lieutenant Governor 154

UNIT 21 Summary 157

UNIT 22 The Municipal Government 159

UNIT 23 Members of the Municipal Government 161

Glossary **164**

GETTING READY TO LEARN

Think about the topics listed in the left-hand column. In the middle column, write what you already know about the topics. Then write three things you want to find out about the topics in the right-hand column.

ABOUT	I ALREADY KNOW	I WANT TO FIND OUT
the federal government		1. _____ 2. _____ 3. _____
the provincial government		1. _____ 2. _____ 3. _____
the municipal government		1. _____ 2. _____ 3. _____

Answer the Questions

1. Have you ever voted in an election? Describe how you voted.
2. Do you think it is important to vote? Why?
3. List three important things you think the government should provide.

Read

What Is a Government?

A government is a group of people who make decisions about how to run a country or an area of land. In Canada there are three levels of government.

The Federal Government

• makes laws for all of Canada

The Provincial Government

• makes laws for the province

The Municipal Government

• makes laws for the municipality

Read

The Federal Government

The **federal** government is the government of Canada. The federal government makes decisions about things that affect all Canadians. It decides about things like immigration, defence, health care and employment. The federal government holds its meetings in Ottawa, Canada's capital city.

The Provincial Government

Canada is too big for the federal government to look after everything. People in different areas of the country have different ideas about what is most important. For example, fishing is very important to people in Nova Scotia, but people in Saskatchewan care more about wheat farming. So each province or territory in Canada has its own government. It is called the **provincial** or **territorial** government.

Provincial governments make decisions only for their own provinces. They decide about things like education, health care and highways. They hold their meetings in the provinces' capital cities.

The Municipal Government

There are hundreds of cities and towns in each province. People in different cities have different concerns. So each city has its own government. **Municipal** government is the government of a city or community. It is sometimes called **local** government.

Municipal governments make decisions only for their own communities. They decide about things like policing, recycling, roads and snow removal.

Understand What You Read

A. Word Meanings

Write the word beside its meaning.

federal • provincial • capital city • local • municipal

1. _____ government of a city

2. _____ government of Canada

3. _____ another name for *municipal*

4. _____ where the government has meetings

5. _____ government of a province

B. Fill in the Blanks

territorial • Ottawa • Canada • federal • provincial • province • municipal

1. The _____ government is the government of Canada.

2. The federal government has meetings in _____.

3. Ottawa is the capital city of _____.

4. The _____ government is the government of a province.

5. The provincial government has meetings in the capital city of the _____.

6. The _____ government is the government of a city.

7. The _____ government is the government of a territory.

C. Circle the Correct Answer

1. The federal government makes decisions for _____.

   a) only one province

   b) the whole country

   c) only one city

2. Each provincial government makes decisions for _____.

   a) only one province

   b) every province or territory

   c) only one city

Understand What You Read

D. True or False

1. Canada has four provincial governments.   T / F

2. Canada has one federal government.   T / F

3. Canada has 10 territorial governments.   T / F

4. Canada has one municipal government.   T / F

5. The Alberta government can make decisions for Ontario.   T / F

E. Crossword Puzzle

Down

1. British Columbia is a _____
4. The _____ government makes decisions only for one province
5. Municipal government is sometimes called _____ government
7. Ottawa is the capital city of _____

Across

2. _____ is the capital city of Canada
3. City government is _____ government
6. The federal government has meetings in _____
8. The _____ government makes decisions for all Canadians

F. Discuss

Look in the blue pages of your telephone book. Find the symbols for the federal government, provincial government and municipal government. Draw a picture of each symbol.

Read

Canada is a **democracy**. A *democracy* means that the people make decisions about their own country.

What Is a Government?

There are many people in Canada. But it is too hard for every person to make decisions about Canada. So we ask a group of people to make decisions for us. This group of people is our **government**. Our government works for all Canadians.

Who Are Politicians?

The leaders of our government are **politicians.** A politician is a person who helps make decisions about how a country is run. There are many people who want to be politicians. We choose the politicians we like by **voting** for them.

This is what makes Canada a democracy. Canadians decide who will govern Canada.

How Do We Choose Politicians?

Canada's government changes every few years. When the government changes, there is an **election.** An election happens when Canadians choose people to govern Canada.

On voting day, we vote by putting a mark beside the name of a **candidate**. We vote only when there is an election. A candidate is a person who wants to be a politician.

We have federal elections, provincial elections and municipal elections. These elections usually happen at different times.

Understand What You Read

A. Word Meanings

Write the correct word beside its meaning.

democracy • politician • election • candidate • government

1. _____ a group of people who make decisions about a country

2. _____ the people make decisions about their own country

3. _____ a government leader

4. _____ a person who wants to be a politician

5. _____ a time when we choose people to govern Canada

B. True or False

1. We can vote whenever we want.   T / F

   _____

2. There is an election every month.   T / F

   _____

3. Democracy means we do not make any decisions about Canada.   T / F

   _____

4. Federal and municipal elections happen at the same time.   T / F

   _____

5. Canada is a democracy.   T / F

   _____

6. The leaders of our government are candidates.   T / F

   _____

Understand What You Read

C. Fill in the Blanks

> years • politicians • election • voting • democracy
> government • people • federal • provincial • municipal

1. Canada is a _____.

2. A democracy means that the _____ decide how their country is governed.

3. Canadians choose _____ to govern Canada.

4. Canadians choose politicians by _____ for them.

5. Canadians vote for politicians when there is an _____.

6. The leaders of Canada's government change every few _____.

7. The _____ changes when there is an election.

8. The government of Canada is the _____ government.

9. The government of a province is the _____ government.

10. The government of a city is the _____ government.

D. Discuss

1. Do you think everyone in Canada votes?
2. Why do you think some people do not vote?

Read

How an Election Works

Every few years the government changes. A government leader calls an election, and tells us the date we can vote for new government leaders.

Once a government leader has called an election, about two months pass before voting day. This time is called the **election campaign.** Many things happen during an election campaign.

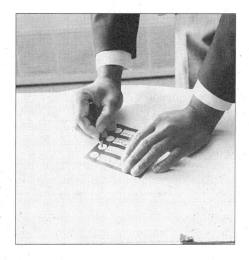

Many **candidates** try to convince you to vote for them. They make speeches. They put their names on signs. They put pamphlets in your mailbox. Sometimes they come to your home.

We listen to the candidates. We ask questions. We try to decide whose ideas we like.

Understand What You Read

A. Answer the Questions

1. Who calls an election?

   _____

2. What is a candidate?

   _____

3. What happens on voting day?

   _____

4. When is the election campaign?

   _____

5. List three things that happen during an election campaign.

   _____

B. Order

Number the sentences in the correct order. Then copy the sentences.

_____ The election campaign begins.

_____ Canadians vote on voting day.

_____ A government leader calls an election.

_____ Candidates try to convince you to vote for them.

1. _____

2. _____

3. _____

4. _____

UNIT 4—How We Vote

Read

Who Can Vote in an Election?

You can vote if you are an **adult** and a **Canadian citizen.** An adult means you are eighteen years or older.

A Canadian citizen means
- you were born in Canada

or

- you became a Canadian citizen

How Do We Vote?

Before voting day, someone visits each home. This person is called an **enumerator.** The enumerator makes a list of all the people who can vote. This list is called the **voters' list.**

If you can vote, the enumerator puts your name on the voters' list. Then you receive a card in the mail. It tells you where to vote on voting day. On voting day you go to the address written on your card.

There you get a **ballot.** A ballot is a piece of paper with the names of candidates on it. You vote in private. You put a mark beside the name of the candidate you like.

Then you put your ballot in the ballot box. At the end of voting day, all the votes are counted. The candidate with the most votes gets **elected.**

Understand What You Read

A. Word Meanings

adult • enumerator • voters' list • ballot • ballot box • candidate

1. _____ what we put our ballots in after we vote

2. _____ a person who wants to be a politician

3. _____ a person who comes to our home before voting day

4. _____ a list of people who can vote

5. _____ eighteen years or older

6. _____ a piece of paper we use to vote

B. Answer the Questions

1. Who can vote in Canada?

   _____

2. What is an enumerator?

   _____

3. How does our name get on a voters' list?

   _____

4. How do we know where to vote on voting day?

   _____

5. What do we do with a ballot?

   _____

6. Where do we put our ballot after we have voted?

   _____

Understand What You Read

C. True or False

1. An adult is someone over sixteen.   T / F

_____

2. A ballot is a list of Canadians who can vote.   T / F

_____

3. A voters' list is a piece of paper with the names of politicians on it.   T / F

_____

D. Order

Number the sentences in the correct order. Then copy the sentences on the lines.

_____ You put your ballot in the ballot box.

_____ An enumerator visits your home.

_____ You get a card in the mail telling you where to vote.

_____ You get a ballot.

_____ You go to the place written on your card.

_____ The enumerator puts your name on the voters' list.

_____ You vote in private.

1. _____

2. _____

3. _____

4. _____

5. _____

6. _____

7. _____

Read

The **federal government** is the government of all of Canada. There is only one federal government in Canada. The leaders of the federal government have meetings in Ottawa, Canada's capital city.

Many people want to be members of the federal government. At election time Canadians listen to the candidates and decide who to vote for.

But Canada is very big. A candidate cannot have ideas for every part of the country. So at election time Canada is divided into 301 areas. Each area has about the same number of people in it. The areas are called **electoral districts.** They are also called **ridings,** or **constituencies.**

Everyone in Canada lives in one of the 301 ridings. At election time, we listen to the candidates from the riding we live in. On voting day we elect one candidate from our riding. So one politician gets elected from each riding.

Some provinces have more people living in them than other provinces. For example, Ontario has more people than any other province. So Ontario is divided into more ridings than the other provinces. This means that every riding has about the same number of people.

THE NUMBER OF FEDERAL RIDINGS IN EACH PROVINCE OR TERRITORY	
Province or territory	**Ridings**
Ontario	103
Quebec	75
British Columbia	34
Alberta	26
Manitoba	14
Saskatchewan	14
Nova Scotia	11
New Brunswick	10
Newfoundland	7
Prince Edward Island	4
Northwest Territories	2
Yukon Territory	1
Canada	**301**

Understand What You Read

A. Circle the Correct Answer

1. Canada has _____ federal government(s).

   a) one

   b) two

   c) 10

2. Canada is divided into _____ federal ridings.

   a) 10

   b) 301

   c) 290

3. Two other names for a riding are _____.

   a) a constituency and a politician

   b) an electoral district and a riding

   c) an electoral district and a constituency

4. Each riding _____.

   a) is the same size

   b) has about the same number of people

   c) is the same size and has the same number of people

5. You can vote _____.

   a) in every riding

   b) in any riding in your province

   c) only in the riding you live in

6. Each riding votes for _____ candidate(s).

   a) 301

   b) 10

   c) one

7. If a province has a high population it has _____ ridings.

   a) more

   b) fewer

Understand What You Read

B. Fill in the Blanks

Write the number of ridings in each province or territory on the map. Saskatchewan is done for you.

C. Answer the Questions

1. How many ridings are in your province? _____

2. How many politicians get elected to the federal government from your province?

    _____

3. How many politicians get elected to the federal government in total? _____

4. Which province do you think has the highest population?

    _____

5. Why do you think this province has the highest population?

    _____

    _____

D. Discuss

1. Do you know the name of the riding you live in?
2. Do you think the riding you live in is bigger or smaller than most ridings in Canada? Why?

Read

Canadians Vote for Members of Parliament

On voting day, we vote for one candidate from the riding we live in. We vote only in our own riding.

Then someone counts the votes in our riding. The candidate with the most votes wins the election. He or she becomes a member of the federal government. We call a member of the federal government a **Member of Parliament.** This is a long name, so we shorten it to **MP**. Sheila Copps is the MP for Hamilton, Ontario.

All 301 ridings in Canada elect MPs this way. So 301 MPs get elected. These MPs form our federal government. Each MP has an office in his or her riding. Each MP also goes to meetings in Ottawa.

Understand What You Read

A. Fill in the Blanks

> **301 • one • Member of Parliament • MP**
> **office • Ottawa • elects**

1. On election day we vote for _____ politician from our riding.

2. We call the elected politician a _____ _____ _____.

3. The short form for a Member of Parliament is an _____.

4. Each MP has an _____ in his or her riding.

5. Canada has _____ federal ridings.

6. Each riding _____ one MP.

7. Each MP goes to meetings in _____.

B. Answer the Questions

Call the federal elections office at 1-800-463-6868 to answer the questions.

1. What is the name of your federal riding?
   (Tell the operator where you live.)

   _____

2. Who is the MP for your riding?

   _____

3. What is your MP's office address and phone number?

   _____

C. Discuss

List three things you could write to your MP about. Choose one and write a letter to your MP.

Read

Where Do Members of Parliament Have Meetings?

MPs have meetings in Ottawa, in the **House of Commons**. There is one seat for each of the 301 MPs in the House of Commons.

What Do MPs Do at These Meetings?

MPs talk about how to govern Canada. They talk about things that concern Canadians. They make laws for Canada.

Here is a picture of the House of Commons. The picture on the bottom is the Parliament Buildings in Ottawa. The House of Commons is inside the middle building. The picture on the top is inside the House of Commons.

Understand What You Read

A. Word Meanings

Write the correct word beside its meaning.

> **House of Commons • Member of Parliament**
> **MP • ridings • electoral district**

1. _____ a member of the federal government

2. _____ short form for a member of the federal government

3. _____ the place where all the Members of Parliament meet

4. _____ areas of land that have about the same number of people in them

5. _____ another name for a riding

B. True or False

Circle T or F. Then write a correct sentence on the line. If the sentence is true, copy the sentence.

1. There are three hundred seats in the House of Commons.   T / F

   _____

2. Ottawa is the capital city of Ontario.   T / F

   _____

3. The House of Commons is inside the Parliament Buildings.   T / F

   _____

4. The Parliament Buildings are in Ottawa.   T / F

   _____

5. There are three hundred MPs.   T / F

   _____

6. MPs make laws only for Quebec.   T / F

   _____

Read

Most Members of Parliament, MPs, belong to a political party.

What Is a Political Party?

A **political party** is a group of people who have similar ideas about how to run the country. There are many political parties. Each political party has a leader.

There are federal political parties and provincial political parties, but usually there are no municipal political parties. Sometimes provincial parties and federal parties have the same name. For example, there are a federal Liberal party and a provincial Liberal party for each province. The federal Liberal party has one leader, and the provincial Liberal party has a different leader.

Here are signs for some of the federal political parties.

At election time candidates will put their names on party signs.

How Can We Find Out Who the Party Leaders Are?

You can find out who the federal party leaders are by calling Elections Canada. If you live in Ottawa, call 954-8584. If you live outside Ottawa, call this toll-free number: 1-800-463-6868. You can also find out who the party leaders are by asking a friend or reading the newspaper.

Understand What You Read

A. Answer the Questions

1. What is a political party?

_____

2. List four different federal political parties.

_____

3. What is the Elections Canada phone number?

_____

B. Fill in the Blanks

Write the names of the federal political party leaders.

FEDERAL GOVERNMENT	
Political party	**Party leader**
Liberal	_____
Bloc Québécois	_____
Reform	_____
Progressive Conservative	_____
New Democratic Party	_____

C. Discuss

What do you think the different political parties would say about topics like health care, jobs, social assistance or education?

Who Is the Prime Minister?

The **prime minister** is the leader of the federal government.

How Do We Choose the Prime Minister?

On voting day each riding elects one MP. So 301 MPs get elected. Most of these MPs belong to a political party. The political party with the most elected MPs becomes the **party in power.** The leader of that political party becomes the prime minister.

The chart below shows how Canadians voted in the 1997 federal election. It shows how many MPs belonged to each party. It also shows the party leaders at the time of the election. Some leaders may be different today.

1997 FEDERAL ELECTION RESULTS		
Political party	**Number of MPs elected**	**Leader of the party**
Liberal	156	Jean Chrétien
Bloc Québécois	44	Gilles Duceppe
Reform	59	Preston Manning
New Democratic Party	20	Alexa McDonough
Progressive Conservative	21	Jean Charest
Other	1	N/A
Total number of MPs	**301**	N/A

Note: *N/A* means not applicable.

The Liberal party had more MPs than the other parties. So the leader of the Liberal party, Jean Chrétien, became the prime minister. The Liberal party became the party in power. The party that comes second becomes the **Official Opposition.**

How Long Will the Liberal Party Be in Power?

The prime minister can call an election any time, but it must be within five years of the election. During the time a party is in power, some MPs or party leaders may retire or quit their jobs.

Understand What You Read

Here is how the ridings in each province voted in the 1993 federal election.

A. Fill in the Blanks

For each province or territory, write the number of MPs elected from the different parties.
Then add up the MPs for each party.

THE NUMBER OF MPs ELECTED IN 1997							
	Liberal	New Democratic Party (NDP)	Progressive Conservative (PC)	Bloc Québécois	Reform	Other	Total
British Columbia	7	4			23		= 34
Alberta							= 26
Saskatchewan							= 14
Manitoba							= 14
Ontario							= 103
Quebec							= 75
Newfoundland							= 7
New Brunswick							= 10
Nova Scotia							= 11
Prince Edward Island							= 4
Yukon Territory							= 1
Northwest Territories							= 2
Total							= 301

Understand What You Read

B. Answer the Questions

Look at the table on page 126.

1. Which party had the most elected MPs in 1997?

   _____

2. Which party became the party in power?

   _____

3. Who became the prime minister in 1997?

   _____

4. Which party became the Official Opposition?

   _____

5. When can the prime minister call another election?

   _____

6. Which province voted for MPs who belonged to the Bloc Québécois party?

   _____

7. How many federal ridings are in Canada? _____

8. How many MPs get elected from each riding? _____

9. How many ridings are in Saskatchewan? _____

10. How many ridings in Saskatchewan elected a Liberal MP? _____

C. True or False

1. Every riding is the same size.   T / F

2. On voting day we vote for a prime minister.   T / F

3. On voting day we vote for an MP.   T / F

4. The prime minister can call an election after six years.   T / F

Understand What You Read

D. Word Meanings

| prime minister • party in power • Official Opposition |
| Member of Parliament |

1. _____ member of the federal government

2. _____ leader of the federal government

3. _____ party with the most elected MPs

4. _____ party with the second-most elected MPs

E. Fill in the Blanks

Find out which party leaders have changed since 1997. Complete the chart.

FEDERAL PARTY LEADERS FOR 1993 (SEE PAGE 125)	FEDERAL PARTY LEADERS TODAY
Liberal _____	Liberal _____
Bloc Québécois _____	Bloc Québécois _____
Reform _____	Reform _____
New Democratic Party _____	New Democratic Party _____
Progressive Conservative _____	Progressive Conservative _____

F. Discuss

1. Which party is in power today?

2. Who is the prime minister today?

3. Do you agree with how our prime minister is governing Canada?

Read

CANADIAN PRIME MINISTERS		
Name of prime minister	Party	Years in power
Sir John A. Macdonald	Conservative	1867 – 1873
Alexander Mackenzie	Liberal	1873 – 1878
*Sir John A. Macdonald	Conservative	1878 – 1891
Sir John Joseph Caldwell Abbott	Conservative	1891 – 1892
Sir John Sparrow David Thompson	Conservative	1892 – 1894
Sir Mackenzie Bowell	Conservative	1894 – 1896
Sir Charles Tupper	Conservative	1896
Sir Wilfrid Laurier	Liberal	1896 – 1911
Sir Robert Laird Borden	Conservative	1911 – 1920
Arthur Meighen	Conservative	1920 – 1921
William Lyon Mackenzie King	Liberal	1921 – 1926
*Arthur Meighen	Conservative	1926
*William Lyon Mackenzie King	Liberal	1926 – 1930
Richard Bedford Bennett	Conservative	1930 – 1935
*William Lyon Mackenzie King	Liberal	1935 – 1948
Louis Stephen St. Laurent	Liberal	1948 – 1957
John George Diefenbaker	Progressive Conservative	1957 – 1963
Lester Bowles Pearson	Liberal	1963 – 1968
Pierre Elliott Trudeau	Liberal	1968 – 1979
Charles Joseph Clark	Progressive Conservative	1979 – 1980
*Pierre Elliott Trudeau	Liberal	1980 – 1984
John Napier Turner	Liberal	1984
Martin Brian Mulroney	Progressive Conservative	1984 – 1993
Kim Campbell	Progressive Conservative	1993
Jean Chrétien	Liberal	1993 – 1997
*Jean Chrétien	Liberal	1997 –

Note: The prime ministers with stars beside their names were in power more than once.

Understand What You Read

A. True or False

Circle T or F. Then write a correct sentence on the line.

1. Canada's first prime minister was Sir Wilfrid Laurier.   T / F

   _____

2. Most prime ministers belonged to the Liberal party.   T / F

   _____

3. Jean Chrétien is Canada's 15th prime minister.   T / F

   _____

   (Some prime ministers were in power more than once. Do not count them twice.)

4. Pierre Elliott Trudeau was in power in 1958.   T / F

   _____

5. There were many New Democratic Party prime ministers.   T / F

   _____

B. Circle the Correct Answer

1. Canada's first female prime minister was _____.
   a) Jean Chrétien
   b) Kim Campbell
   c) Alexander Mackenzie

2. A picture of Sir John A. Macdonald is on Canada's _____-dollar bill.
   a) five
   b) 50
   c) 10

3. Jean Chrétien belongs to the _____ party.
   a) Reform
   b) Progressive Conservative
   c) Liberal

UNIT 11—The Cabinet

Read

The prime minister is the leader of the federal government. But he or she has a difficult job. So the prime minister chooses some MPs to give him or her advice. The MPs the prime minister chooses are called **cabinet ministers.**

What Do Cabinet Ministers Do?

Each cabinet minister advises the prime minister on a **ministry**. A ministry is a part of the government. There are usually between 15 and 25 ministries. Here are four ministries.

> **Ministry of Citizenship** • **Ministry of Transportation**
> **Ministry of Immigration** • **Ministry of Justice**

The prime minister decides how many ministries and cabinet ministers there will be.

What Is the Cabinet?

The prime minister and the cabinet ministers are called **the cabinet.**

What Does the Cabinet Do?

The cabinet discusses laws it wants to make for Canada. A **law** is a rule everyone has to follow. When the prime minister and cabinet ministers agree on an idea they want to become a law, they write it down. They call it a **bill**.

A bill describes a new law. It is called a bill because it is not yet a law for Canadians. The bill can be about how to tax Canadians, how to spend government money, what Canadians cannot do, or many other topics.

The cabinet presents the bill to the rest of the MPs in the House of Commons. The MPs decide if they like the bill. They discuss the bill. Then they vote on the bill.

Understand What You Read

A. Answer the Questions

1. Who are cabinet ministers?

   _____

2. Who chooses cabinet ministers?

   _____

3. What do cabinet ministers do?

   _____

4. What is a ministry?

   _____

5. Name two ministries.

   _____

B. Circle the Correct Answer

1. The prime minister and the cabinet ministers are the
   - cabinet
   - House of Commons

2. The cabinet writes
   - laws
   - bills

3. The cabinet presents the bills to the
   - House of Commons
   - the prime minister

4. An MP who advises the prime minister about a ministry is a
   - cabinet minister
   - cabinet

Understand What You Read

C. Fill in the Blanks

| House of Commons • bills • law • prime minister • votes |

1. The _____ and the cabinet ministers are called the cabinet.

2. A bill describes a new _____.

3. The cabinet writes _____.

4. Then the cabinet shows the bills to the _____.

5. The House of Commons _____ on the bill.

D. Crossword Puzzle

Across

1. The leader of the House of Commons
3. Made up of all the MPs
5. Describes a new law

Down

2. A part of government
4. The prime minister and cabinet ministers
6. A rule for Canadians

Read

How Does a Bill Become a Law?

The cabinet presents a bill to the House of Commons. The MPs in the House of Commons listen to the bill. They discuss it. Sometimes they do not agree on the bill and they change it. Then they vote on the bill. If most of the MPs vote for the bill, the bill usually becomes a law for Canada. But first **the Senate** must vote for it.

What Is the Senate?

There are two main parts to our federal government.

First, there is the **House of Commons.** All the MPs we elected are in the House of Commons. The prime minister and cabinet ministers are also MPs.

Second, there is **the Senate.** The Senate is made up of as many as 112 people chosen by the prime minister. These people are called **senators**. In 1997, the Senate has 104 senators.

Here is a picture of the Senate. It is in the Parliament Buildings in Ottawa. It looks like the House of Commons, but it is smaller.

What Does the Senate Do?

The Senate votes on a bill after the House of Commons has voted for it. The Senate either votes for the bill or tells the MPs to change it.

If the Senate votes for the bill, the Governor General signs the bill. Then it becomes a law for Canada.

Understand What You Read

A. Word Meanings

Write the correct word beside its meaning.

> **House of Commons • the cabinet • the Senate • a bill • a law
> a senator • cabinet ministers • a ministry**

1. _____ 104 people called senators

2. _____ the place where MPs meet

3. _____ the prime minister and cabinet ministers

4. _____ a rule for Canadians

5. _____ a person in the Senate

6. _____ describes a new law

7. _____ some MPs who advise the prime minister

8. _____ Ministry of Immigration

B. Answer the Questions

1. What are the two main parts of the federal government?

   _____

2. When does the Senate vote on the bill?

   _____

3. What happens after the Senate has voted for the bill?

   _____

4. Who chooses senators?

   _____

Read

Who Is the Governor General?

The Queen of England is the official head of our government. Her name is Queen Elizabeth II. But she does not live or work in Canada. So someone who lives in Canada does her job. This person is called the **Governor General**. Our present Governor General is Roméo Le Blanc.

What Does the Governor General Do?

The Queen and the Governor General do not govern Canada. Canadian politicians govern Canada. They make laws. Then the Governor General signs the laws to make them legal. The Governor General also introduces new governments.

How a Bill Becomes a Law

First the cabinet writes a bill.
Next the cabinet presents the bill to the House of Commons.
Next the House of Commons votes on the bill.
Then the Senate votes on the bill.
Then the bill becomes a law when it is signed by the Governor General.

Understand What You Read

A. Order

Number the sentences in the correct order. Then copy the sentences.

_____ The Senate votes on the bill.

_____ The cabinet writes a bill.

_____ The Governor General signs the bill to make it a law.

_____ The House of Commons votes on the bill.

_____ The cabinet presents the bill to the House of Commons.

1. _____

2. _____

3. _____

4. _____

5. _____

B. Fill in the Blanks

Elizabeth II • bills • Queen of England • law • Governor General

1. The head of our federal government is the _____.

2. The Queen's name is Queen _____.

3. The _____ does the Queen's job in Canada.

4. The Governor General signs _____.

5. When the Governor General signs a bill, it becomes a _____.

C. Answer the Question

Who is Canada's Governor General?
(You can call Elections Canada at 1-800-463-6868 to find out.)

_____

Write the missing information.

(You can call Elections Canada at 1-800-463-6868)

FEDERAL GOVERNMENT	
Governor General:	_____
Party in Power:	_____
Prime Minister:	_____
Official Opposition:	_____
Official Opposition Leader:	_____
My Federal Riding:	_____
My Member of Parliament:	_____
My MP's Address:	_____
My MP's Phone Number:	_____

Read

A **provincial government** is the government of a province. A **territorial government** is the government of a territory.

There are 10 provincial governments and two territorial governments in Canada. Each province has its own provincial government, and each territory has its own territorial government.

What Does the Provincial Government Do?

Each provincial government makes decisions for the people in its own province. The provincial governments also make laws for their provinces.

How Do We Elect Members of the Provincial Government?

Each province or territory has its own election. These elections are usually held at different times. For example, Ontario had an election in 1995, and Alberta had an election in 1993.

Each province is divided into **ridings.** These are also called *electoral districts*. Each riding has about the same number of people in it. Each riding in a province elects one politician to the provincial government.

For example, Ontario is divided into 130 provincial ridings. Each riding elects one politician. So 130 politicians form Ontario's provincial government.

Everyone in the province votes on the same day.

Are Provincial Ridings the Same as Federal Ridings?

Provincial ridings are different from federal ridings. We live in a federal riding that has one name and a provincial riding that has a different name.

Understand What You Read

A. Fill in the Blanks

Canada • ridings • 10 • province • two • different

1. There are _____ provincial governments in Canada.

2. There are _____ territorial governments in Canada.

3. The federal government makes laws for all of _____.

4. The provincial governments make laws only for their own _____.

5. Each province is divided into _____.

6. Federal ridings and provincial ridings are _____.

B. Answer the Questions

1. How many ridings does Ontario have?   _____

2. How many politicians do the people in each riding elect?   _____

3. How many politicians are in the Ontario government?   _____

4. What is another name for a riding?

   _____

5. Can the Ontario government make a law for Alberta?   _____

6. Can the federal government make a law for Alberta?   _____

7. Does every province have its provincial election on the same day?

   _____

Understand What You Read

Each province is divided into a number of ridings. Each riding has about the same number of people in it.

Here is a picture of an imaginary province called *Glat* to help you understand ridings. Imagine Glat has one hundred people living in it. Each circle on the map is a person. There are ten ridings. Each riding has 10 people in it.

Divide the map into 10 ridings. One riding is drawn for you.

C. Answer the Questions

1. Are the ridings the same size? _____

2. Does each riding have the same number of people in it? _____

3. The people in each riding will elect one politician to the government. How many politicians will form the government? _____

4. If everyone moves to the north of Glat,

   a) will every riding still have 10 people in it? _____

   b) will we need to change the size of the ridings? _____

Every five years the government of Canada has a census. Then we find out how many people have moved. Sometimes the size of our ridings or the number of our ridings changes. For example, in 1985 Ontario had 125 provincial ridings. By 1995 Ontario had 130 provincial ridings.

Read

On voting day we vote for a candidate from the riding we live in. We can vote only in our own riding. Then someone counts the votes in our riding. The candidate with the most votes becomes a member of the provincial government.

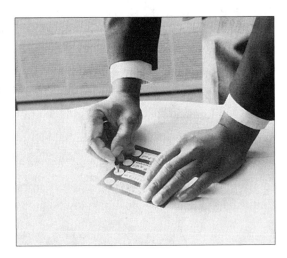

Each riding in the province elects a member of the provincial government on the same day. These members form the provincial government. Each member has an office in his or her riding. Each member also goes to meetings in the capital city of the province.

What Are Members of the Provincial Government Called?

In different provinces the provincial government and the members of the provincial government are called different names. In most provinces the provincial government is called the **Provincial Parliament** or the **Legislative Assembly**. Here is a list of the different names.

NAMES FOR PROVINCIAL GOVERNMENTS AND THEIR MEMBERS			
Province	The provincial government	Member of the provincial government	Short form
Some provinces	Legislative Assembly	Member of the Legislative Assembly	MLA
Some provinces	Provincial Parliament	Member of the Provincial Parliament	MPP
Quebec	National Assembly	Member of the National Assembly	MNA
Newfoundland	House of Assembly	Member of the House of Assembly	MHA

Read

Where Do the MPPs Have Meetings?

MPPs have meetings in the capital city of their province. Every province or territory has a building where the provincial government leaders meet.

For example, here are photos of two government buildings. The photo at the top is the government building in Toronto, Ontario. It is called *Queen's Park*. The photo below is the government building in Victoria, British Columbia. It is called the *Parliament Buildings*.

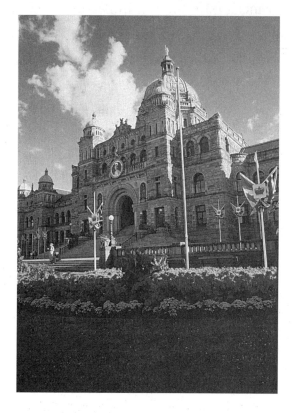

Understand What You Read

A. Fill in the Blanks

Write the short form beside the correct word.

> **MNA • MHA • MLA • MPP • MP**

1. Member of the House Assembly   _____

2. Member of the Provincial Parliament   _____

3. Member of the National Assembly   _____

4. Member of the Legislative Assembly   _____

5. Member of Parliament   _____

B. Circle the Correct Answer

1. An _____ is a member of the federal government.
   a) MPP
   b) MLA
   c) MP

2. There are _____ provincial governments in Canada.
   a) 10
   b) two
   c) one

3. Members of the provincial government have meetings in _____.
   a) Canada's capital city
   b) Ottawa
   c) the capital city of a province

4. Most provinces call a member of the provincial government an _____ or an _____.
   a) MNA/MPP
   b) MPP/MLA
   c) MHA/MLA

5. In your province, a member of the provincial government is called an _____.
   a) MPP   c) MNA
   b) MLA   d) MHA

Understand What You Read

C. Fill in the Blanks

Write the city in which each provincial or territorial government has meetings.

British Columbia _____

Alberta _____

Saskatchewan _____

Manitoba _____

Ontario _____

Quebec _____

Newfoundland _____

New Brunswick _____

Nova Scotia _____

Prince Edward Island _____

Yukon Territory _____

Northwest Territories _____

D. Answer the Questions

You can call the elections office for your province or territory (see page 146).

1. What is the name of your provincial riding?

_____

2. Who is the member of provincial government for your riding?

_____

3. What are the address and phone number of your MPP's office?

_____

_____

Elections Office Phone Numbers

Here is the phone number of the elections office for each province or territory.

Some phone numbers have a 1-800 before them. They are **toll-free** numbers. *Toll-free* means you do not pay for the phone call, even if it is long distance.

Most toll-free numbers only work if you are calling from within the province. So if you are calling from outside the province, you have to dial the number on the right.

If you live in the same city as the elections office, do not dial the 1-800 number.

PHONE NUMBERS FOR ELECTIONS OFFICES		
Province or territory	**Dial this toll-free number if** **• you live in the province**	**Dial this number if** **• you live outside the province** **• or you live in the city listed**
British Columbia	1-800-661-8683	604-**387-5305** (Victoria)
Alberta	—	403-**427-7191** (Edmonton)
Saskatchewan	—	306-**787-4000** (Regina)
Manitoba	1-800-282-8069	204-**945-3225** (Winnipeg)
Ontario	1-800-668-2727	416-**321-3000** (Metro Toronto)
Quebec	1-800-461-0422	418-**643-5380** (Quebec City)
Newfoundland	—	709-**729-0712** (St. John's)
New Brunswick	1-800-308-2922	506-**453-2218** (Fredericton)
Nova Scotia	1-800-565-1504	902-**424-8584** (Halifax)
Prince Edward Island	1–888–234–8683	902-**368-5895** (Charlottetown)
Yukon Territory	—	403-**667-5200** (Whitehorse)
Northwest Territories	1-800-661-0796 (toll-free Canada-wide)	403-**920-6140** (Yellowknife)

Elections office phone numbers were published with the permission of the elections offices.

UNIT 17—Political Parties

Read

Most members of the provincial government belong to a political party.

You can call the elections office (see page 146) for your province or territory to find out the leaders of the political parties.

Write the political parties and party leaders for your province or territory. Then write the names of the federal political parties and party leaders.

PROVINCIAL GOVERNMENT	
Political party	**Party leader**
_____	_____
_____	_____
_____	_____
_____	_____
_____	_____
_____	_____

The phone number of the elections office for your province or territory is _____.

FEDERAL GOVERNMENT	
Political party	**Party leader**
Liberal	_____
Bloc Québécois	_____
Reform	_____
New Democratic Party	_____
Progressive Conservative	_____
_____	_____

The phone number of the elections office for the federal government is 1-800-463-6868.

Read

Who Is the Premier?

The **premier** is the leader of the provincial government.

How Do We Choose the Premier?

On voting day each riding in the province elects a member of the provincial government. After the election we find out how many members belong to each party. The party with the most members becomes the **party in power**. The leader of that party becomes the premier.

Sometimes a member of the provincial government does not belong to any political party. He or she is called an **independent**.

For example, here are Ontario's 1995 election results.

ONTARIO'S 1995 ELECTION RESULTS		
Political party	**MPPs elected**	**Party leader**
Progressive Conservative	82	Mike Harris
Liberal	30	Lyn McLeod
New Democratic Party	17	Bob Rae
Independent	1	N/A

The Progressive Conservative party, or PC, had more MPPs than the other parties. So the leader of the PC party became the premier of Ontario. The PC party became the party in power.

How Long Will the PC Party Be in Power?

The premier can call an election any time, but it must be within five years of the last election.

Understand What You Read

A. Fill in the Blanks

1. The premier is the leader of the $\Big\langle$ federal / provincial $\Big\rangle$ government.

2. In a provincial election we vote for $\Big\langle$ the premier / the prime minister / an MPP

3. The party in power has $\Big\langle$ the most / the second-most $\Big\rangle$ elected MPPs.

B. True or False

1. The premier can call an election after two years.   T / F

   _____

2. The premier is the leader of the party in power.   T / F

   _____

3. The premier is the leader of the provincial government.   T / F

   _____

4. On voting day we vote for a premier.   T / F

   _____

5. On voting day we vote for a member of the provincial government.   T / F

   _____

6. Every province has 10 premiers.   T / F

   _____

Understand What You Read

Each province in Canada has its own provincial government led by a premier. The chart below lists the provinces.

Write the names of the premiers and the parties in power. You can find their names by reading the newspaper, phoning the provincial elections office (see page 146) or asking a friend.

The premiers will change from time to time. Usually, each province calls an election at a different time.

C. Fill in the Blanks

PROVINCE	PREMIER	PARTY IN POWER
British Columbia	_____	_____
Alberta	_____	_____
Saskatchewan	_____	_____
Manitoba	_____	_____
Ontario	_____	_____
Quebec	_____	_____
Newfoundland	_____	_____
New Brunswick	_____	_____
Nova Scotia	_____	_____
Prince Edward Island	_____	_____

Who is the premier for your province? _____

Read

The premier is the leader of the provincial government. But he or she has a difficult job. So the premier chooses some MPPs to give him or her advice. The MPPs he or she chooses become **cabinet ministers.**

What Do Cabinet Ministers Do?

Each cabinet minister advises the premier on a provincial **ministry**. A ministry is a part of government. Here are four provincial ministries.

> **Ministry of Finance** • **Ministry of Education**
> **Ministry of Social Services** • **Ministry of Transportation**

The premier decides how many provincial ministries there will be.

What Is the Cabinet?

The premier and his or her cabinet ministers are called **the cabinet.**

What Does the Cabinet Do?

The cabinet discusses laws it wants to make for the province. When members of the cabinet agree on a law, they write it down. They call it a **bill.**

Then the cabinet presents the bill to the rest of the MPPs. The MPPs listen to the bill and talk about it. Then they vote on the bill. If most of the MPPs vote for the bill, the lieutenant governor signs the bill. It becomes a law for the province.

The provincial government works almost like the federal government. But there is no Senate in the provincial government.

Understand What You Read

A. Answer the Questions

1. What do cabinet ministers do?

   _____

2. Who chooses cabinet ministers?

   _____

3. What are two provincial ministries?

   _____

4. What is a ministry?

   _____

B. Circle the Correct Answer

1. The cabinet is
   - the premier and the cabinet ministers
   - the cabinet ministers and the MPPs

2. The cabinet writes
   - bills
   - laws

3. Then the cabinet presents the bills to the
   - MPPs
   - premier

4. An MPP who advises the premier about a ministry is a
   - ministry
   - cabinet minister

5. The provincial government
   - has
   - does not have
   a Senate

6. The provincial government
   - has
   - does not have
   a prime minister

Understand What You Read

C. Word Meanings

Write the correct words beside their meanings. You will find the words on page 151.

1. _____ the leader of the provincial government

2. _____ The premier chooses some members of government to

    give him or her advice. They are _____.

3. _____ the premier and his or her cabinet ministers

4. _____ a member of the provincial government

5. _____ a rule for Canadians

6. _____ describes a new law

D. Crossword Puzzle

Across

1. They advise the premier
2. It is a ____ before it is a law
4. A part of government
6. The _____ government has a Senate

Down

1. The premier and cabinet ministers
3. A provincial ministry
5. The leader of the provincial government
7. Each province has a _____ government
8. The provincial government does not have a _____

Read

How Does a Bill Become a Law?

First the cabinet writes a bill.
Next the cabinet presents the bill to the rest of the members of the provincial government.
Next the members of the provincial government vote on the bill.
Then the bill becomes a law when it is signed by the **lieutenant governor**.

Who Is the Lieutenant Governor?

The Governor General does the Queen's job for the federal government. There is also someone who does the Queen's job for each provincial government. We call this person the *lieutenant governor.* There are 10 lieutenant governors. There is one in each province.

The person who does the Queen's job in the territories is called the **commissioner.** There are two commissioners.

What Is the Queen's Job?

The Queen's job is to sign bills after the members of government have voted for them. This makes the bills into laws for Canadians.

The Queen lives in England, so the Governor General, lieutenant governors and commissioners do her job in Canada. Hilary Weston is Ontario's lieutenant governor.

Understand What You Read

A. Order

Copy the sentences in the correct order.

- The cabinet presents the bill to the members of the provincial government.
- The lieutenant governor signs the bill to make it a law.
- The cabinet writes a bill.
- The members of the provincial government vote on the bill.

1. _____

2. _____

3. _____

4. _____

B. Circle the Correct Answer

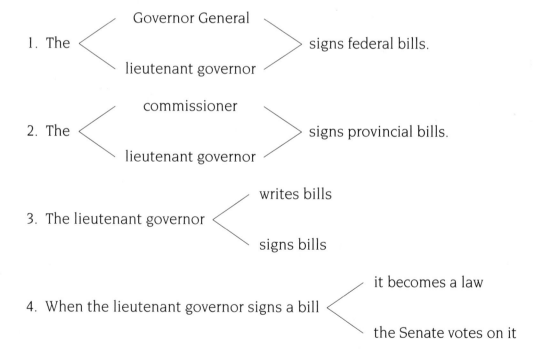

1. The ⟨ Governor General / lieutenant governor ⟩ signs federal bills.

2. The ⟨ commissioner / lieutenant governor ⟩ signs provincial bills.

3. The lieutenant governor ⟨ writes bills / signs bills ⟩

4. When the lieutenant governor signs a bill ⟨ it becomes a law / the Senate votes on it ⟩

C. Answer the Question

Who is the lieutenant governor for your province?

_____

Understand What You Read

D. Sort

Write the words under *Federal* or *Provincial*. Two words will be used twice.

> cabinet ministers • cabinet • lieutenant governor
> Governor General • MPs • MPPs • premier • prime minister
> House of Commons • Senate

FEDERAL	PROVINCIAL
_____	_____
_____	_____
_____	_____
_____	_____
_____	_____
_____	

UNIT 21—Summary

Complete the missing information.

PROVINCIAL GOVERNMENT	
Provincial Government for	_____
Lieutenant Governor:	_____
Party in Power:	_____
Premier:	_____
Official Opposition:	_____
Official Opposition Leader:	_____
My Provincial Riding:	_____
My MPP:	_____
My MPP's Address:	_____
My MPP's Phone Number:	_____

PROVINCIAL GOVERNMENT FOR _____	FEDERAL GOVERNMENT

Shade your province.

Lieutenant governor	_____	Governor General	_____
Party in power	_____	Party in power	_____
Premier	_____	Prime minister	_____
Official Opposition	_____	Official Opposition	_____
Official Opposition leader	_____	Official Opposition leader	_____
My provincial riding	_____	My federal riding	_____
My MPP	_____	My MP	_____
My MPP's address	_____	My MP's address	_____
My MPP's phone number	_____	My MP's phone number	_____

Read

The **municipal government** is the government of a city, town, village or community. A **municipality** is a town, city, village or community. Each municipality in Canada has its own government.

Another name for municipal government is **local government**.

What Does a Municipal Government Do?

Members of the municipal government make decisions for the people in their own municipality. They make **bylaws**. A bylaw is a law made by the municipal government.

The municipal government makes decisions and bylaws about things like policing, fire protection, jails, roads, hospitals, water and schools.

Do We Elect Members of the Municipal Government?

We elect members of the municipal government during municipal elections. These usually happen at a different time from provincial or federal elections. The people who live in each municipality decide who will be members of their municipal government.

Most municipalities are divided into smaller areas of land called **wards.** Each ward has about the same number of people in it. The people who live in each ward elect members of the municipal government for their ward.

Understand What You Read

A. Fill in the Blanks

List six things the municipal government makes decisions about.

1. _____ 3. _____ 5. _____

2. _____ 4. _____ 6. _____

B. Circle the Correct Answer

1. In Canada there are _____ of municipal governments.

   a) 10

   b) two

   c) hundreds

2. Another name for municipal government is _____ government.

   a) local

   b) municipality

   c) territorial

3. A municipality is divided into voting areas called _____.

   a) ridings

   b) wards

   c) municipalities

Read

The City of Toronto is divided into 28 wards.

The people in each ward elect two members of municipal government to represent them.

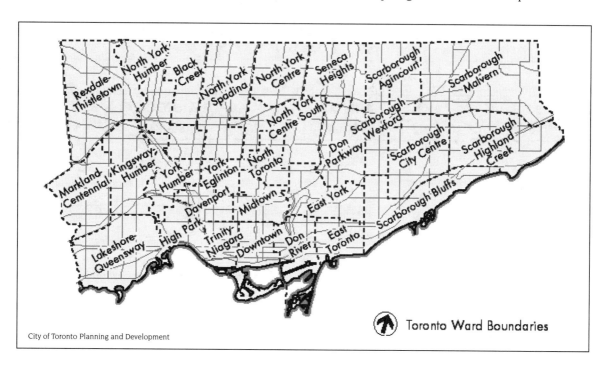

Toronto Ward Boundaries

City of Toronto Planning and Development

What Are Members of the Municipal Government Called?

Municipal governments work differently in different provinces, so it is hard to explain everything about them.

The municipal government in most cities is called the **council.** The people from each ward elect a **councillor.** A councillor is sometimes called an *alderman* or *alderwoman*.

For the City of Toronto, the city council is made up of 56 councillors. There are two councillors from each ward. The people in the municipality also elect a leader of council. The leader is called a **mayor.** In some municipalities, the leader is called a *reeve*.

Most municipalities also elect **school board trustees** to make decisions about local schools.

Understand What You Read

A. Sort

Write the words under *Federal*, *Provincial* or *Municipal*. Use the words in the box.

> council • premier • 10 • one • Canada • MPP • mayor
> prime minister • councillor • hundreds • Parliament
> MP • city • Legislative Assembly

FEDERAL GOVERNMENT	PROVINCIAL GOVERNMENT	MUNICIPAL GOVERNMENT
_____	_____	_____
_____	_____	_____
_____	_____	_____
_____	_____	_____
_____		_____

B. Fill in the Blanks

> council • bylaws • mayor • reeve • councillors • alderman or alderwoman

1. The leader of the municipal government is the _____.

2. Members of the municipal government are called _____.

3. Another name for a mayor is a _____.

4. Another name for a councillor is an _____.

5. The municipal government makes _____.

6. The municipal government is called the _____.

C. Answer the Questions

1. What is the name of your municipality?

2. Who is the mayor for your municipality?

3. Who is the councillor for your ward?

Understand What You Read

D. Fill in the Blanks

Write *municipality, province* or *country* beside each place in the list below.

1. _____ Toronto

2. _____ Ontario

3. _____ Canada

4. _____ Victoria

5. _____ Alberta

6. _____ St. John's

7. _____ Charlottetown

8. _____ Canada

9. _____ Manitoba

10. _____ Nova Scotia

11. _____ Winnipeg

12. _____ Quebec

F. Discuss

1. List three city bylaws.

2. If you were mayor in your municipality, what bylaws would you pass about parking?

GLOSSARY

Adult:	A person eighteen-years-old or older.
Alderman or alderwoman:	A municipal politician, sometimes called a *councillor*.
Ballot:	A piece of paper with the names of candidates for voting.
Ballot box:	A box our ballots go into after we have voted.
Bill:	Describes a new law.
Bylaw:	A municipal law.
Cabinet:	The federal cabinet is the prime minister and cabinet ministers.
	The provincial cabinet is the premier and cabinet ministers.
Cabinet ministers:	Members of government the prime minister or premier chooses to advise him or her on an area of government.
Candidate:	A person who enters an election campaign to become a member of government.
Commissioner:	The Queen's representative in the territories.
Constituency:	A riding.
Councillor:	A municipal politician.
Democracy:	When people make decisions about their own country.
Election:	A time we vote for new members of government.
Election campaign:	A time candidates try to convince us to vote for them.
Electoral district:	A riding.
Enumerator:	A person who visits our homes to make a list of voters.
Federal government:	The government of Canada.
Governor General:	The Queen's representative in Canada.
House of Assembly:	The name for the provincial government in Newfoundland.
House of Commons:	The place where MPs meet.
Independent:	A candidate for government who does not belong to a political party.
Law:	A rule Canadians must obey.
Legislative Assembly:	The name for the provincial government in some provinces.
Lieutenant governor:	The Queen's representative in each province.
Mayor	The leader of the municipal government.
MHA	Member of the House of Assembly.

Ministry:	Department of the government.
MLA:	Member of the Legislative Assembly.
MNA:	Member of the National Assembly.
MP:	Member of Parliament.
MPP:	Member of Provincial Parliament.
Municipal government:	Government of a city, town or community.
Municipality:	A city, town or community.
National Assembly:	The name of the provincial government in Quebec.
Official Opposition:	The political party with the second-most elected members of government.
Party in power:	The political party with the most elected members of government.
Politician:	A member of government.
Premier:	The leader of the provincial government.
Prime minister:	The leader of the federal government.
Provincial government:	The government of a province.
Provincial Parliament:	The name of the provincial government in some provinces.
Reeve	The leader of the municipal government in some cities.
Riding:	A voting area.
Senate:	A part of the federal government.
Senators:	People chosen by the prime minister who belong to the Senate.
Territorial government:	The government of a territory.
Toll-free:	When you do not pay for a long-distance telephone call.
Vote:	To put a mark on your ballot beside the name of the candidate you want to elect.
Voters' list:	A list of the people who can vote.
Ward:	A municipal voting area.